The Best-Kept
[SECRETS]
of Parenting

18 PRINCIPLES THAT CAN
CHANGE EVERYTHING

BRAD WILCOX AND JERRICK ROBBINS

D1042641

Published by Familius™ LLC, www.familius.com

Familius books are available at special discounts for bulk purchases for sales promotions, family, or corporate use. Special editions, including personalized covers, excerpts of existing books, or books with corporate logos, can be created in large quantities for special needs. For more information, contact Premium Sales at 559-876-2170 or email specialmarkets@familius.com

Library of Congress Catalog-in-Publication Data
2014931018
pISBN 978-1-938301-40-7
eISBN 978-1-938301-39-1
Printed in the United States of America

Edited by Brooke Jorden
Cover Design by David Miles
Book Design by Brooke Jorden

10 9 8 7 6 5 4 3 2 1
First digital edition 2014
First Edition

[ACKNOWLEDGEMENTS]

We are grateful for the opportunity we've had to write this book and for all who have helped in the process. We would especially like to thank the individuals at Familius—Christopher Robbins, Brooke Jorden, Maggie Wickes, David Miles, and the rest of the design and marketing team—for the countless hours they've spent editing and designing this book.

Thanks also to the many people who contributed to the book by letting us share their examples and stories. Thanks to our friends who supported us and taught us about following our dreams, including Sally White, Hal and Barbara Jones, and Robert Parker. And finally, a big thank you to our own families, whose love supported us through this process—especially Debi Wilcox, Aimee Robbins, and Rob and Liz Robbins. We are overjoyed to be striving toward family happiness with you by our sides.

[AUTHORS' NOTE]

Dear parent,

What you are about to read, if applied, will change everything! The pages that follow contain eighteen secrets of parenting that will increase family unity, family happiness, and family communication. We hope to be helpful guides on the road to a stronger family. As a parent whose children are grown and out of the home and an adult who's just moved out of the home, we've combined the perspectives of a parent raising children and a child being raised to assemble these secrets. Allow us to introduce ourselves:

Hello, I'm Brad Wilcox. I am a professor in the Department of Teacher Education at Brigham Young University where I also work with youth programs such as Especially For Youth. I taught sixth grade in Provo before obtaining my PhD in Education at the University of Wyoming.

My wife Debi and I have four children and four grandchildren. Our family has lived for a time in New Zealand and also in Chile.

I am the author of *Straight Talk for Parents: What Teenagers Wish They Could Tell You* and *Tips for Tackling Teenage Troubles*. I have spoken on the topic of effective parenting to groups across the United States, Europe, Australia, and Japan.

Reading, writing, teaching, and traveling are some of my favorite endeavors. I love peanut M&Ms and pepperoni pizza, but I realize that's not too healthy, so I'm trying really hard to learn to like salads.

Hi, I'm Jerrick Robbins. Welcome to *The Best-Kept Secrets of Parenting*! I have to admit, I felt very apprehensive at first about approaching this topic since I'm not yet a parent. However, I have two wonderful examples in my mom and dad; they showed me by their actions how to raise a family. I'm the oldest of seven children spread out over seventeen years. As a teenager, I watched how my parents interacted with my younger siblings with great interest—mostly for information I could use to get out of doing chores later that week. Instead of accomplishing that admittedly self-serving motivation, I learned to appreciate the way my parents taught, disciplined, and communicated with their children. I learned firsthand the benefits of good parenting because I was the beneficiary of good parenting.

I'm originally from a city called Henderson, Nevada. Many of my grandparents, aunts, uncles, and cousins lived close by while I was growing up, which provided me with even more great examples of parents trying hard to help their families grow closer together. I love all sports, but in high school I settled on volleyball and still love playing it. Singing in choirs, reading good books, spending time with my family, and fiddling around with architecture are some of my favorite hobbies. I will soon finish my Bachelor's degree in English at Brigham Young University.

We—as authors of this book—sincerely believe that these eighteen principles can help you and your family achieve greater family happiness. We have seen these principles change everything for our families, and they can do the same for you. Whatever stage of life you're in with your family, there is something for you in this book. We hope you enjoy it!

Best wishes,

Brad & Jerrick

[CONTENTS]

[INTRODUCTION]

A few years ago, during the hot summer month of July, Jerrick's family—he, his parents, and six younger siblings—were attempting to drive from Las Vegas to Colorado Springs in only one day. Take nearly twelve hours of uninterrupted time in the car together, complete with restless toddlers and another child prone to motion sickness, and you have the recipe for an unforgettable family trip!

The bags were finally packed, and somehow—miraculously—they all fit into the Suburban along with the children. The family pulled out of the driveway only a couple of hours behind schedule. Fifteen minutes into the drive, the customary chant began: "Mom . . . Dad . . . Are we there yet?" That was shortly followed by calls of "I'm hungry," "Mom, he's touching me," "Luggage is falling on my head," and "She's not wearing her seatbelt." And of course there was the constant bickering between children about the temperature in the car being either too hot or too cold.

One particular child, Trevor, a ten-year-old boy with lots of energy and a passion for pestering, began wreaking havoc. This was his dream situation—all his siblings were within arm's reach, unable to escape his torturous teasing. In his mind, Christmas had come early. After a few attempts at pulling his sister's hair without Dad noticing, Dad noticed. "Hands to yourself!" he bellowed from the driver's seat.

Not to be distracted from his goal, Trevor realized that not only was everyone in the family within reach, they were also within earshot. He

1

immediately began a beautiful rendition of his favorite tune: "Oh, I'd love to be an Oscar Mayer wiener, then everyone would be in love—with—me!" He continued to repeat the song over and over again until Mom wished she could give everyone in the car earplugs.

Amidst groans and whines from the other children, Dad's voice pierced the fray. "OK Trevor, everyone, quiet game. One, two, three—go."

Due to the family's competitive nature, there was blessed silence for approximately five seconds, followed by the loveable voice of energetic Trevor calling out, "I lost! Oh, I'd love to be . . . " The tears of laughter that simple statement initiated impaired Dad's vision so much that an accident almost occurred. The next eleven hours were more of the same, but despite all the obstacles, the family safely made it to their destination.

Family life can be much like this road trip—unpredictable and full of challenges, problems, and laughter along the way. We might even feel a little carsick because of all the twists and turns in the road. As we navigate life's potholes, we may often think, *Are we there yet? Is this trip ever going to end?* However, there are some secrets that can make getting there more predictable with fewer challenges. The following pages cover eighteen of these secrets, from using the roadmap of effective communication to the short-cuts of alleviating negative stress and pressure. They remind us to refuel by maintaining positive attitudes and a long-term perspective. To help, we've included principles of action at the end of each chapter. These principles of action include questions that can help you examine the progress your family has made in your journey. Our hope is that the information, stories, and advice contained in this book will help you map your road to family happiness.

[SECRET #1]

LAUGH A LOT

Some time ago, Brad was a passenger on an airplane that was coming in for a landing. As they neared the airport, he and the other passengers started to realize that they were traveling much faster than normal. Brad could feel the anxiety level in the plane start to rise.

Suddenly, the airplane hit the ground with great force and then began taxiing down the runway. Shaken, the passengers sat in stunned silence until the captain's voice came over the sound system: "Take that, you bad, bad runway!" All the passengers erupted in laughter. With a humorous viewpoint and a shared laugh, an uncomfortable situation became bearable.

Teenage Eli was helping his dad with some family shopping at the grocery store. While pushing the cart toward the car, he decided to have a little fun and take a ride. He pushed off and coasted on the back of the cart until his weight tipped the whole thing upside down and he ended up flat on his back underneath a pile of broken eggs and smashed tomatoes. Eli expected his father to yell and become angry, but instead, his dad started laughing hysterically.

Today's families face serious challenges and troubling problems, but humor can help. Humor can heal. Humor can raise the pain threshold, lower a fever, reduce stress, and improve the body's immune system.

Along with these physical benefits, humor also offers social and emotional benefits. Any environment without humor can be a grim, lonely, and fearful place, but when you add humor, the environment changes. Humor is valuable not just in aesthetic aspects of life but in everything. It can play a role in all facets of learning and living. The secret is simple: Families can choose to use humor to improve perspectives, strengthen relationships, and cope with struggles. Positive humor can strengthen commitment, cohesiveness, appreciation, and affection. And those who feel they are at a disadvantage in the humor department can take heart in knowing that a sense of humor can be developed.

[HUMOR CAN IMPROVE PERSPECTIVE]

We can't always choose what we look at, but we can choose what we see. One brother and sister were yelling and arguing when their dad rushed into the room. "Where are the cats?" he asked loudly, frantically looking around.

"Dad, there aren't any cats in here," the kids said.

Their father just shook his head and said, "I could have sworn I heard two cats fighting up here." Dad's comment diffused the situation and helped the siblings see their behavior from a different perspective. Instead of resuming their fight, the kids started laughing.

Another example of how humor helps us keep perspective occurred when a little boy asked his teacher to help him find his coat. The teacher said, "It's right over there on the hook."

The boy responded, "No. That's not mine."

The teacher then joined the boy in looking around the classroom and playground. Finally, they returned to the coat rack and the teacher asked, "Are you sure this isn't your coat?"

"Yes, I'm sure," said the boy. "Mine had snow on it!"

Seeing the humor of the situation helped the teacher keep a good perspective, and when she later shared it with the child's parents, they enjoyed a good laugh, too.

[HUMOR CAN STRENGTHEN RELATIONSHIPS]

Abraham Lincoln related beautifully with others by using humor. Once, during a political debate, it is said that a rival called Lincoln "two-faced." Lincoln simply responded by saying, "I leave it to my audience. If I had another face, do you think I'd wear this one?"[i]

Like Lincoln, parents and children can use humor as a positive way to relate to each other. Public speakers know that a funny story or joke can break the ice and make listening and learning more palatable. We need to remember that humor can play the same role in our homes. It can help parents get our points across without being too preachy or overbearing.

Early in their marriage, James learned that his new wife habitually read in bed before going to sleep. Occasionally, he would come into the bedroom and find Liz asleep with a book in her hands. He would carefully put the book on the nightstand, gently take off her glasses, and turn off the light—until the night she looked up and said groggily, "I wanted to finish that book, but I just kept falling apart."

Now, more than twenty years later, "falling apart" is still used as a substitute for "falling asleep" in James and Liz's family. The right twist on the English language, dropped into a tense moment, can invite parents and children to crack up with laughter, and that laughter bonds them in a powerful way. One high school student received a B- on an English paper and decided he would attempt to soften the teacher up. Since

Valentine's Day was approaching, he purchased a big, heart-shaped box of chocolates with the words "Be Mine" written across the front. The student left the gift on his teacher's desk in hopes of improving his grade, but didn't have much luck. The note he received back from the teacher said simply: "Thanks for the delicious candy, but it is still a Be Mine-us." The grade wasn't changed, but the relationship between the teacher and student was strengthened.

[HUMOR CAN HURT]

While humor can be used to build relationships, it can also hurt them—especially when not everyone is laughing. Family members must be careful to distinguish between genuine humor, which everyone can enjoy, and hurtful humor, which is at someone else's expense. The resulting wounds can go deep. Many people remember mean comments for years, and the very relationships which should be the most meaningful in our lives may be damaged or destroyed. A hasty "just kidding" doesn't excuse rude jokes or sarcasm. Ridiculing others in an effort to make ourselves feel superior is a misuse of humor.

A young man once attended a youth dance in a different state. The friend who invited him began introducing him to a group of girls standing near the door as they entered. Since the visitor didn't know anyone, he was anxious to make some points with the ladies, so he said, "Wow. There sure are a lot of beautiful girls in your state." His friend looked around the group and, trying to be funny, said loudly, "Where? Where? I don't see any." Needless to say, those boys were not the most popular guys at the dance that night.

If the above experience had been a scene on a TV show, the friend's "clever" comment would have been followed by laughter. In reality, the girls were offended and avoided the boys the rest of the evening.

Television producers use a laugh track—prerecorded laughter that can be turned on and off at the touch of a button. That's why laughter always follows sarcastic put-downs. It sounds like everyone enjoys the negative humor. In real life, there is no laugh track. People might put up with put-downs and manage a chuckle for the sake of saving face, but deep down, negative humor hurts. No matter how perfect the timing or how smoothly executed the joke, usually the only ones laughing are those who are afraid they may be the next targets.

One young woman went home feeling deflated and unimportant almost every night after being around a certain young man in her group of friends. He constantly made fun of, criticized, and belittled her. When asked why she continued to spend time with him, she responded, "He says I have to learn how to take a joke. I figure it's not worth losing friends over." Why does she continue to be around this hurtful guy? And why does he think he's so funny in the first place? How sad that this girl has to cope with her friend rather than genuinely enjoying his company.

We should be able to joke around with our family, but there is a big difference between having fun by joking and making fun through joking. Family members should help you feel better about yourself. They don't try to make themselves feel better at your expense. Family members should enjoy mutual trust as much as they enjoy a good laugh. Home should allow you to let your guard down instead of always requiring you to keep your defenses up.

Humor perceived as controlling ("Keep laughing and you'll be laughing all the way to your room!") or sarcastic ("You're so graceful" after a family member trips) can hurt relationships and create an atmosphere of defensiveness instead of closeness. Family members then may not trust one another to be gentle and to protect each other from harshness or unkindness. Moreover, parents who can't laugh at their own faults and are angry when their children notice parental imperfections may convince children that adulthood is humorless and grim and that parents and other authority figures have lost the ability to be compassionate.

Family members usually know each other's weaknesses and fears. When mutual respect is present, they don't treat those fears lightly or make jokes about another's weakness. The love in a family is diminished by "humor" that makes another want to withdraw. Appropriate humor unifies the family with warmth, laughter, and a desire to be together. Appropriate humor helps families make it through anything.

[HUMOR CAN HELP US COPE]

Two adult sisters were devastated when their mother, age fifty-three, died after a long illness and hospitalization. But their aunt, after an especially bleak day of traveling and making funeral arrangements, began to tell stories about their mother, and the sisters remembered funny and sweet stories of their own. Soon they were all laughing and crying at the same time, and their loss became more endurable.

Susan and Joe, with their family of six small children, had been vacationing in Mexico. Joe's work required him to return to their home in Wyoming a few days early, and Susan, pregnant with number seven, found herself shepherding her brood through customs and having to deal with mounting distractions and problems. "There I was," she recalls, "out of money and out of diapers. I was trying to keep track of all the luggage and all the children at the same time. I was so pregnant I could hardly walk." The man at the customs counter looked from Susan to her six noisy charges and back to Susan. "Lady, go right on through," he invited. "If you have any drugs in those bags, you need them." A humorous viewpoint, a shared laugh, and Susan's journey became bearable.

We all encounter things that seem inconvenient, terrible, or even intolerable. We change what we can, but sometimes we simply have to accept and cope with unpleasant circumstances. Humor can be a helpful coping tool.

After Art E. Berg was thrown from an automobile during a rollover just five weeks before his wedding date, his neck was broken, and at the age of twenty-one, he was left a quadriplegic. Although his body no longer served him as it once did and he was confined to a wheel chair, Art was far from being helpless and depressed. He lived a life full of service, activity, and accomplishment. What got him through? Among other things, Art realized that peace came from learning to laugh again, particularly with his family. He wrote, "I am not sure I would have survived the emotional trauma of my injuries and the complications of my new life if it hadn't been for the wit, chuckles, laughs, and good-natured humor of my wife and family."[ii]

Abraham Lincoln struggled with depression and used humor as therapy. Of Lincoln, Russell Freedman wrote: "He was certainly a humorous man, famous for his rollicking stories. But he was also moody and melancholy, tormented by long and frequent bouts of depression. Humor was his therapy. He relied on his yarns, a friend observed, to 'whistle down sadness.'"[iii]

[A SENSE OF HUMOR CAN BE DEVELOPED]

Barbara Barrington Jones confirms, "Believe it or not, humor can be developed. I am living proof of that fact."[iv] Barbara's father was an accountant, and her mother taught etiquette in a private girls' school; her home was quiet and orderly, and decorum reigned. But when Barbara grew up, she found that decorum wasn't necessarily a cure for all of her needs. When she began speaking, consulting, and writing, her first attempts were, as she described them, "disasters" because she couldn't break out of the serious mindset with which she had been raised.

Lacking a personal background of humorous experiences, Barbara began searching for humor. She started keeping a notebook in which she wrote down funny things she experienced or heard. For example, she attended a conference in which a speaker told of a letter that a man received from a child after undergoing heart surgery: "I know that you will be OK because in the Bible it says 'Blessed are the pacemakers.'" With a smile, Jones wrote this incident down in her notebook. Another heartfelt touch of humor was mentioned by another man who described a handmade get-well card he received while recovering from bypass surgery. On the front of the card, his grandchild, a second grader, had drawn a long, rectangular black box, representing a coffin, with a long flower poking out of the center. Inside, the grandchild had printed in big letters, "Hope you get well soon, but if not, have fun." After a hearty laugh, Barbara wrote down that account as well. Thanks to her notebook, Barbara collected a number of examples she could use in her own presentations and writings and, at the same time, sharpened her ability to recognize and appreciate humor.

Like Barbara Barrington Jones, as humorous situations arise in our homes, we need to take a moment to enjoy them and even record them instead of just letting them pass. This is what one mother did when her daughter announced, "I think we should all make get-well cards for McKenzie. She's in the hospital because her independence burst."

Another mother remembers when Santa visited with young Tanner and asked, "Have you been a good boy?"

"Well," Tanner replied honestly, "I've been a little mean."

Santa began to laugh as Tanner continued, "But not as mean as my friend Jacob. Santa, you'll know his house because he has a gray roof."

And Brad remembers when, at his young daughter's request, his family was playing restaurant and his daughter was taking their orders. "I'll have a hamburger," Brad said.

"You can't, Dad," she said in disgust. "This is a Chinese restaurant. You have to have spaghetti or lasagna."

We can follow the example of Barbara Barrington Jones and start our own humor notebooks. When we expect ourselves to record, collect, and share examples of humor, we will learn to watch for funny moments and savor them. That's a personal way each of us can work on developing our own sense of humor.

Sharing jokes during meal times can be a positive experience. Once children are introduced to a joke genre, let them try their hands at creating their own riddles and knock-knock jokes. You'll be surprised at how many new ways you can invent for the chicken to cross the road or for someone to change a light bulb.

Sharing family stories is another surefire way to evoke laughter. "Remember when Uncle Chris took Uncle Roger's stash of candy and thought no one would notice?" "Remember when Whitney fell and hurt her chin so many times and she said, 'If my chin gets hurt once more I think it's going to say it quits being on my face!'" "Remember when Dad hadn't shaved and David felt his face and said, 'Wow, Dad, your freckles are sharp!'"

When parents help children notice, read, write, collect, remember, and share humor in their lives, they are helping them develop a valuable skill that will allow them to keep a good perspective, relate with others, and cope with problems. When humor starts becoming negative, parents can insist that laughter be used only to lift.

At first glance, laughter and the seriousness of our lives might seem incompatible. After all, helping our family members grow and develop is serious business! However, the secret is that when we find a place for humor in our lives, it can create flexibility and creativity within ourselves, build bridges between people, and strengthen family relationships. So go ahead and develop that sense of humor. It's an important part of a healthy family and happy home. Humor helps and heals, so go ahead and laugh.

On their road trip to Colorado, Jerrick and his siblings often asked, "Are we there yet?" In your own family journey toward happiness, you may also find yourself asking, "Are we there yet?" The answer is that our trip together as a family is just beginning. We may still have a long road ahead, but having a sense of humor is one secret that will help us find joy along the way.

[PRINCIPLES OF ACTION]

How can you use humor to improve family happiness? Here are some suggestions:

» **Humor Can Improve Perspective:** Think of a time when you've been cheered up by humor. How can you improve someone else's perspective by using appropriate humor?

» **Humor Can Strengthen Relationships:** Think of a family member whom you wish to grow closer to. How can humor bring you closer to that family member?

» **Avoid Hurtful Humor:** When have you seen the negative effects of hurtful humor on someone's life? Now imagine the positive effects that genuine humor could have on that individual.

» **Humor Can Help Us Cope:** Think of a happy, humorous memory about a family member who has passed away. How has that memory helped you cope with losing that family member?

» **A Sense of Humor Can Be Developed:** Do you consider yourself to be genuinely humorous? If not, what can you do to develop your sense of humor?

UMBACH Lewis, Jason Michael

390651375
24466
Transited:
June 22,
2019 11:15
AM

[ENDNOTES]

i. Russell Freedman, *Lincoln: A Photobiography* (New York: Clarion, 1987).

ii. Art Berg, *Finding Peace in Troubled Waters: 10 Life Preservers for When Your Ship Springs a Leak* (Salt Lake City: Deseret Book, 1995), 100.

iii. Russell Freedman, *Lincoln: A Photobiography* (New York: Clarion, 1987), 4.

iv. Barbara Barrington Jones, *The Confident You* (Salt Lake City: Deseret Book, 1992), 139.

MAKE FRIENDS WITH YOUR FAMILY

B rad loved his parents until he entered seventh grade. Then he found out it wasn't cool to love your parents. He remembers hearing other students talk about how mean, unfair, and old-fashioned their parents were, and he decided that if he planned to survive in this new environment, he had better start hating his parents. So he hated them. It wasn't as easy as he first thought it would be, because he really loved them, but a man's gotta do what a man's gotta do.

All the way home on the bus, he tried to hate them. All the way up his long driveway, he told himself he hated them. He flopped down in front of the TV and reminded himself to hate them. But he just couldn't hate his mom and dad when he was watching *The Brady Bunch*. He decided to go outside to the field behind his house where he could hate his parents properly.

Between his house and the field was a barbed-wire fence. All his life he had gone under the fence, but now, being a man, he determined to go over the fence. He grabbed the top of the rough wooden fence post with his right hand and began climbing the barbed wire until he straddled the fence with one leg on each side. At that moment Brad thought, *This is about the dumbest thing I've ever done.* Suddenly, the barbed wire on which he was balancing gave out. He landed forcefully on the fence, and the jagged wooden post shot through his right hand—yes, in one side and out the other. Brad's first thought was not *I hate my parents.* He began yelling for his mom and dad as loudly as he could. He did not care if they were at the South Pole, they were going to hear him!

Brad's dad was driving up the driveway. He heard Brad screaming and rushed to the fence. He pulled Brad's hand off the post, wrapped it in a dish towel, and hurried him to the hospital emergency room. Not once did Brad think, *I can't stand this guy. He doesn't like my music. He doesn't like my hair.* Not once did he think, *I am going to be so embarrassed if any of my friends see me with my dad.* And he sure didn't think, *My dad is so old-fashioned to still believe in emergency rooms!* On the contrary, Brad felt grateful that his dad was there and was willing to help him when he got himself into such a ridiculous mess.

The entire time the doctor stitched Brad's right hand back together, his dad sat next to him, holding his left hand and squeezing it over and over. Brad said, "I'll never forget the love I felt from my dad that day— the very day I had decided I was going to hate him."

As children grow up and strive for independence, it is natural for them to sometimes react negatively to parents and other family members, as Brad did in seventh grade. Children often begin to see that, contrary to childlike opinions, their parents and siblings aren't perfect. Children begin to see human foibles that can sometimes overshadow the good qualities within their parents. Think back to when you became a teenager, and think about the struggles you faced as you tried to establish your independence from your parents. It is a difficult balancing act that can often lead to hurt feelings and other unintended consequences.

We must strive to keep the sometimes less-than-perfect actions of family members, especially our children, in perspective. Are the things that bother us deliberate or unintentional mistakes? Might we see such actions differently if we thought about the many pressures that they face? Most family members are doing the best they can, but we all still make mistakes. We should learn to forgive family members just as we hope they would forgive us.

Some of us hold in our minds a picture of family perfection. The picture portrays wonderful, dedicated parents surrounded by grateful, obedient children all smiling happily together. Their home swells with wholesome music. Each evening they gather together to enjoy their nutritious dinner, and even the youngest children engage in stimulating discussions. Everyone exercises daily, completes chores happily, says "I love you," and comes out of dental check-ups without a single cavity.

While such a picture is nice as an ultimate ideal, it is far from realistic or essential. Jerrick can't remember a time where his family came out of the dentist without a single cavity, but that's OK. No matter how far from that ideal our own families may be, such differences do not need to hinder our personal progress towards being friends with our family. That's the secret!

One of Jerrick's favorite children's books was *A Light in the Attic*, a collection of poems by Shel Silverstein. In the poem "How Many, How Much," the question is asked, "How much love inside a friend?" The answer is, "Depends how much you give 'em."[i] We have control over how much we value the friendship of our family members. Even in difficult circumstances, we can still be friends with our family even if they aren't so friendly toward us.

One girl wrote, "My father is a transvestite. He doesn't live with us anymore, but you have no idea how much what he does affects me." A young man wrote, "My dad left my mother several years ago because he chose to live a homosexual lifestyle. I fake like it doesn't bother me, but deep down it eats at me every hour I'm awake." Another boy wrote, "My mother always abused us, not physically but mentally and emotionally. She manipulated my sisters and me by making us feel totally worthless." A young woman explained, "My older brother abused me sexually for years." Those experiences leave deep emotional scars in the victims that are often left unresolved and create problems later when those people have families of their own. How do we deal with parents, siblings, and children that don't treat us nicely or deliberately misuse our friendship? The answer to this question is often personal and never easy. It may take many years to resolve the deep hurt, anger, and frustration that come when our family members treat us with disregard.

A young college student wanted to learn more about this topic because of struggles she had faced with her family. She searched carefully through many books and magazines but found little. She said, "There's a lot of counsel on how to be a good parent and have a good family, but very little has been written on what to do with a bad family." She is correct. Responding to dysfunctional family members is a sensitive issue that has not been frequently addressed, perhaps because such situations and relationships are usually so complex and unique that advice of a general nature offers little help. But if the issue is not addressed at all, those whose family members are involved in negative behavior and abuse may misunderstand the silence and suppose that no one is aware of or even cares about their pain. They may mistakenly assume that they are the only ones dealing with such challenges.

We share the following principles to offer some perspective and hope—especially on down days. The principles apply to both parents struggling with wayward children and parents struggling with how they were treated by their own family in the past. We realize this advice is far from complete, but regardless of the situations in our lives over which we have no control, each of us can seek to become friends with our families by applying the secrets of learning, lifting, and loving.

[THE SECRET OF LEARNING]

Part of Brad's professional responsibilities for a time included super-vising student teachers in their public school assignments. One young woman was extremely frustrated because the co-operating teacher to whom she had been assigned was definitely not going to be winning any teaching awards in the near future. During one of Brad's visits, the student teacher pulled him aside to comment on dozens of things she felt that the classroom teacher was doing wrong.

Admittedly, Brad had to cringe at some of the out-of-date practices of the co-operating teacher, but with all the professionalism he could muster, he reminded the student teacher that she was a guest in that teacher's classroom and encouraged her to worry about only her own performance.

Several days later, Brad checked back. To his surprise, the student teacher seemed happier.

"Has the teacher improved?" he asked her privately.

"No," she replied, "but I have discovered that I can learn just as much from a bad example as I can from a good one." Like this student teacher, those in negative situations at home can still learn positive lessons.

A boy we'll call Mike acquired this technique of learning from a bad example in his home. Mike grew up with a dictatorial father he felt he could not please. Mike was continually being compared with his broth-ers and coming up short. It seemed that nothing he did was good enough for his father. To make matters worse, Mike's father had a sharp temper, and any disagreement usually ended in a heavy-handed whipping.

As Mike grew up, he promised himself that when he had children of his own, he would not repeat his father's mistakes. Mike determined that although he could not change what had happened with his father in the past, he could learn from the experiences. Coming from a dys-functional home did not mean he had to be dysfunctional himself.

Mike married, had children, and remained true to his private promises made as a teenager. Mike was sensitive to his children's feelings. He accepted their individual differences and did not compare them with each other. He praised positive behavior, and when a child's behavior was not so positive, he talked to that child privately rather than exploding in front of everyone as his father had done. Remembering how he craved approval and affection as a child, he hugged and kissed his own children daily and attended one child's musical concerts as often as he attended another's sports events.

Now, many years later, children and grandchildren who have been blessed by Mike's good example are thankful that he learned so much from a bad one. Mike explained, "Let any cycle of negative behavior stop with you. That's what I tried to do. It hasn't always been easy, but when I felt sorry for myself, it helped to look around and see that others were also dealing with less-than-perfect family circumstances. I knew many people who were finding a great deal of joy in their lives despite their parents' problems."

A good friend will help us become better people. Although Mike's father wasn't friendly toward him, Mike still tried to be friends with his father by learning from him, and he was a great friend to his own children and grandchildren because of it.

A woman we'll call Rita remembers the problems she caused her parents when she was a teenager. At one point, she even moved out of the house and in with a friend because of one particularly vulgar disagreement with her mother. "I learned a lot from that experience about myself," she said, "and when I returned to my family, I came with a better attitude and appreciation for what my parents did for me. It was still difficult as a teenager having to live under their house rules, but it was now bearable."

Later, Rita got married and had children of her own. When her eldest daughter began to rebel, Rita was able to use the things she learned from her own rebellion against her parents and keep things in perspective. When our children disobey and disrespect us, it will do us a lot of good to remember that we were young once, as well. Look back on those times, remember the lessons you learned as a teenager, and try to put yourself in your children's shoes so you can see the situation from all sides and know how to best love and serve your children.

No one in dysfunctional family circumstances would ever wish the same on another soul. Still, we can take great comfort in knowing that others—like Mike and Rita—who have had to deal with similar trials have been able to transcend them and have determined to make life better for their posterity. As we seek to learn, we can draw strength and courage from their experiences.

[THE SECRET OF LIFTING]

One student at college asserted, "The idea is not to get a whiteboard and teach formal lessons to family members. The idea is to quietly be the best example you can be." She is correct. The most effective way of lifting and teaching in a family setting is through example.

We cannot be expected to be accountable for the actions of others, but we can hold ourselves responsible for our own actions. One of the best ways that we can honor our families is by living our lives the best we can.

"But what if your family doesn't want your good example?" wrote one girl. "The rules in my house were to smoke, drink, yell, and swear. The reward I received for being an example by not doing those things was for my parents to kick me out and my siblings to pretend they didn't know me."

There are too many who can relate to this girl's words. Brad and his wife have a dear friend who married with her parents' strong disapproval. She did not want to hurt her mother and father by going against their wishes, but she knew that she needed to make the right choice for herself. Her parents had warned her she would be disowned if she married her husband, and they made good the threat. It was difficult, but the friend remained true to her decision and moved forward with wedding plans. Not only did her parents choose not to attend, they sent letters to all friends and relatives who had been invited to the reception telling them not to attend or send gifts.

Such behavior hurt the newlywed couple deeply. They felt like saying, "Well, if that's the way you're going to be, then fine. If you don't want anything to do with us, we don't want anything to do with you either." But this couple knew that however natural the tendency to return hate for hate and however justified we may sometimes feel in seeking revenge, these efforts are ultimately wasted.

The young couple knew that if they truly wanted to lift their parents, they would have to stay on higher ground, regardless of the pain, unfairness, and hurt involved. Happily, this couple decided, "Our parents may shut us out of their lives right now, but we will not shut them out of ours." They phoned her parents weekly, just as they phoned his parents.

Another blow came when the young couple announced their first baby. Her parents said that since they did not acknowledge her wedding, in their eyes this baby was illegitimate. Still, the couple continued to stand on higher ground. This couple was setting an example, and although her parents don't want to see it right now, the example these two were offering had the power to one day bring the family back together, stronger than ever before. They were choosing to be friends with their parents, even though their parents didn't want to be friends with them at that moment.

The same holds true when our children decide to go against our wishes. Some of Jerrick's friends, whom we'll call Chris and Dianne, have a child named James who decided to leave home as a teenager. He became wrapped up in illegal substances, was thrown in jail, and lost contact with his family.

Once he was out of jail, James contacted his family and expressed to them how sorry he was to have treated them that way. Chris and Dianne welcomed their son back into the family with open arms. He quit smoking, cleaned up his appearance, and started looking for a job. However, one day, James took one of the family's vehicles and left without saying a word. Months later, the family discovered that James became involved with drugs again, wrecked the car, and was once again incarcerated. Rather than disowning their child, Chris and Dianne keep trying to contact James and offer words of encouragement to him, all the while hoping that one day he will decide to change his life for the better.

It's not always easy to stay on higher ground. One of our heroes is the great educator Booker T. Washington, an African-American born into slavery who lived through a time of intense prejudice and hatred. Yet he lived by this rule: "I shall allow no man to belittle my soul by making me hate him."[ii]

A young man named Don was in a home situation where conversations consisted mostly of put-downs, dirty jokes, swear words, and less-than-subtle innuendoes. Don realized the atmosphere was polluting him in ways that were affecting him emotionally. When he heard himself start to laugh at the jokes and join in the put-downs, he decided to make a change—not in his living arrangements, but in his attitude. He knew he had little control over the language of his parents and siblings, but he could control whether he would join them. In that way, he chose to be on higher ground where he could lift them with his example.

Walter Dean Myers, an author of bestselling young adult fiction, said "cutting people out of your life is easy, keeping them in is hard."[iii] But doing hard things is worth it. Lifting with our example is one way to stay friends with our family, or to try and create a friendship where none exists.

[THE SECRET OF LOVING]

A young man from Nevada had a rough stepfather who was disappointed in his stepson because of the boy's interests. He enjoyed art, music, and reading rather than sports, cars, and rowdy parties. This stepfather saw those interests as a weakness and was actually upset that this teenager wouldn't prove his manhood by fighting, drinking, and chasing girls. When the boy was eighteen, his stepfather kicked him out of the house. He was invited to stay at the home of a friend.

He wrote this letter once: "I know I should feel love for my parents, but I wonder how I will ever be able to love my stepfather when I don't even like him very much." In time, the boy realized that loving someone doesn't mean he had to spend a lot of time with him, emulate him, or follow him when he's wrong. At that point, loving his stepfather could mean feeling sorry for him and not giving up hope that one day he might change.

The same question this boy asked could be repeated by the parents of children who have disassociated themselves from the family. "I know I should feel love for my child, but I wonder how I will ever be able to love him when I don't even like him very much." The answer to this question is the same answer that this boy found over time. Loving our children doesn't mean we have to spend a lot of time participating in their actions, encouraging them to continue on their current wayward path, or condoning their bad decisions. At that point, loving our children could mean not giving up hope that one day they might change.

Regardless of whether or not children change, emotional maturity is taking responsibility for our own actions and feelings, regardless of the choices of others. We can't say, "I'm mad and it's my son's fault" or "I'm sad and it's my daughter's fault." As difficult as it can be, we must be in charge of our own feelings. It is not everyone else's job to change so we can be happy. We are in charge of our own happiness.

Do your remember Jerrick's family's trip to Colorado? A few hours into the trip, one of his siblings got sick to his stomach and vomited in the car. The smell was awful, and everyone at that point was thinking, *Are we there yet?* Although a few members of the family weren't feeling very friendly toward that child at the moment, the family pulled over and because they loved that child they lifted him not only out of the car seat to clean it, but they also lifted his spirit by finding humor in the situation. In your family journey, you may also be asking, "Are we there yet?" The secret is that making an effort to be friends with our family will make the ride more enjoyable. No matter what other family members do, we can develop the secrets of learning, lifting, and loving them. Our feelings of friendship toward them will grow, and hopefully those feelings will be reciprocated. However, even if they aren't, our efforts at friendship can strengthen us during rough roads in the journey because we know we're taking responsibility for our own feelings and doing our best to be friends with our family.

[PRINCIPLES OF ACTION]

How can you become friends with your family? Here are some points to keep in mind:

» **The Secret of Learning:** Think of a family member who has overcome difficult circumstances in his or her life. What can you learn from that example?

» **The Secret of Lifting:** What traits and talents do you have that you can use to lift specific family members around you? How can they be applied more often?

» **The Secret of Loving:** How have your feelings of friendship with your family strengthened you in times of difficulty? How can you increase those feelings?

[ENDNOTES]

i. Shel Silverstein, "How Many, How Much," in *A Light in the Attic*, (New York: Harper Collins, 1981), 8.

ii. Booker T. Washington, *A New Treasury of Words to Live By*, Ed. William Nichols (New York: Simon and Schuster, 1947), 132.

iii. Walter Dean Myers, *Slam!* (Scholastic, 1996).

[SECRET #3]

LEARN TO COPE WITH PRESSURE AND STRESS

"I wish my parents would try to understand how really hard it is for a teenager nowadays," writes Tristen from Tennessee. "It's hard to be everything we're expected to be with all the peer pressure there is to drink, to break family rules, and to even break the law. Sometimes kids would rather be dead than different. And then we are pushed at home to get good grades and be responsible around the house. Sometimes it's so hard that I just want to lie down and forget about it."

Do children have pressure and stress in their lives? The answer is a resounding yes! So do adults! What pressures? There are as many different answers to this question as there are people who feel pressured. But, quite simply, pressures are any external force that influences us. Such forces may come from friends, school, media, the Internet, and any change in our lives, however minor. Stress is an internal reaction to those outside pressures, and stress affects our health and happiness.

It is important to remember that although we usually speak of pressure and stress in negative ways, they are a vital part of our lives. Positive pressure (or eustress) can help us progress and improve. The kind of stress and pressure that good friends and family create in our lives can push us to accomplish goals that we otherwise wouldn't attempt.

For example, from his great-grandfather on down, every male member of Jerrick's family earned their Eagle Scout awards. The award signifies the completion of many merit badges and service projects designed to help a young man develop qualities of love, selflessness, and dedication. The culminating Eagle Scout project is a combined two hundred–hour service project that benefits the community. It was important to Jerrick and his parents that he earned this award because of the qualities he would develop while accomplishing it and because he didn't want to break the streak his great-grandfather started. When Jerrick turned sixteen, the freedom of driving caused him to be a bit unmotivated in other aspects of his life. Even though he had worked very hard up to that point to earn his Eagle Scout award, he began to procrastinate completing his Eagle Scout project to the point that his parents worried he never would finish it. Jerrick's mom was afraid that he—as the oldest great-grandchild—would break that streak and consequently break his great-grandfather's heart.

"You don't want Great-Grandpa Wursten to be disappointed in you, do you?" Jerrick's mom would constantly ask him.

Jerrick looked up to his great-grandpa and didn't want to let him down. As a result of the pressure and stress that those constant reminders created on Jerrick, he earned his Eagle Scout award just before the age cutoff of eighteen, keeping the family streak alive.

Stress can keep us motivated and productive. It often allows us to concentrate, focus, and perform at peak efficiency. Without it, we would likely become pretty bored and frustrated.

Pressure and stress are unavoidable facts of life. The way we handle them is what makes such experiences positive or negative. When the heat is on, do we see it as a refiner's fire or just let it burn us out?

Remember the movie *The Wizard of Oz*?[i] Dorothy found herself traveling a road that led through an unfamiliar world. She encountered many challenges and problems, but she also found three friends to share the journey and help her find her way home—the Scarecrow, the Tin Man, and the Lion. Many of our children are in much the same situation as Dorothy and are looking to build a support system to help them deal with their challenges. We can be that support system for our children just like the Scarecrow, Tin Man, and Lion were for Dorothy.

In the movie, the Scarecrow wanted a brain, which would help him think; the Tin Man wanted a heart, which would allow him to feel and show emotions; and the Lion wanted courage, which would make him brave. Only through their journey to find those attributes were the Scarecrow, Tin Man, and Lion able to help Dorothy find her way home. As we help our children deal with pressure and stress, we must learn to think things through and manage our own stress appropriately. We must learn to exhibit emotions associated with the heart, and we can find personal courage to face problems through learning about and emulating worthy heroes. The secret is that as we learn to deal with our stress, we can be in a better position to help our children deal with theirs.

[GET A BRAIN]

When Brad was in graduate school, he and his wife often felt overwhelmed. As they mapped out one week's schedule, they frequently said, "OK, we'll just have to take it one thing at a time." They chuckled one evening when their daughter, who was in fourth grade then, pulled her homework out of her backpack and sighed, "I'll just have to take it one thing at a time."

The secret of thinking through a problem and generating solutions does not always come naturally. It takes experience and practice to break a problem down into parts, focus on the most important parts first, and then solve the problem, one step at a time. How many of us think about the consequences of our actions ahead of time? Everyone loves to watch fireworks on the Fourth of July, but few consider that, on the fifth of July, someone has to clean up the mess.

Do you realize that simply by not drinking or smoking, people already have a huge jump on others when it comes to stress management? Some of the best ways to reduce stress are to stop smoking and to limit your intake of caffeine and alcohol.

There are also other ways to deal with stress. Do we know how to relax by taking a break? Do we know how to appropriately escape for a while and have some fun? Do we know how to organize our time? Many of the pressures that come up and cause stress in our lives might be avoided with a little advanced planning.

[HAVE A HEART]

Everyone feels emotions, but many learn to bottle them up rather than expressing them appropriately. One of the best secrets of managing stress is being able to express what you're feeling.

Jerrick remembers a time during high school when he learned that bottling up emotions isn't healthy. When he was a freshman, he decided to try out for the volleyball team at his high school. He took classes at a local rec center, played whenever he had the opportunity, and eventually was put on the school's "B" team roster—the freshman team. The team that year was exceptional, but Jerrick wasn't. In fact, even with all the classes he took, Jerrick still hadn't learned to control his body enough to get a serve over the net.

There were many freshmen on the team that year, and as a result, Jerrick rarely got to participate in team practices and he never played during the games. Half way through the season, he had an extended ailment that didn't allow him to participate in athletic activity. Jerrick remembers his coach that year telling him that it wouldn't be beneficial to try out for the sophomore team the next year because he wouldn't make it.

That statement really hurt Jerrick emotionally, but he used it as motivation to work even harder. Aided by a growth spurt, Jerrick eventually became one of the better players on the varsity team, but he still harbored an unspoken grudge towards his "B" team coach for never believing in him.

His senior year, the program made a coaching change, and Jerrick's old "B" team coach became his new varsity coach. Jerrick had never spoken with the coach about his feelings, and that created an unneeded dynamic of stress within the team. Eventually, that stress boiled over, and Jerrick couldn't keep it in any longer. He approached his coach before a game and respectfully told him how the grudge he felt was holding him back. The coach calmly listened to Jerrick, and the two talked and resolved their differences. Both individuals made apologies, and they were able to move on.

During their conversation, Jerrick and his coach both used appropriate language and were still able to express their emotions effectively. Hurtful emotions—like the ones Jerrick felt towards his coach—don't need to be expressed in hurtful ways. Even though there were times during that season when Jerrick wished he could yell at his coach, he refrained. Our need to express emotions does not give us the right to be unkind or hurtful. We may want to yell, "You stupid idiot, why did you do that?" We would be wise to instead send a message focused on "I" instead of "you," such as "I feel frustrated when you do that."

It may also be wise to vent by writing in a journal. A journal can provide a safe place for us to express emotions honestly and openly when we feel we simply can't deal with offenders face to face.

[TAKE COURAGE]

Managing the things that cause us stress can be scary. Looking at a page and a half of tasks that cause us stress and trying to conquer it can be daunting to anyone. When we learn the secret of taking courage, we can look at that task list with confidence.

One of the most effective ways to learn courage is from worthy heroes. Who are the heroes we look up to? When asked, many people might report that their top idols are the Beatles, Elvis Presley, Katy Perry, or Tiger Woods, all of whom have made questionable life decisions in the past.

No wonder one young woman said, "Being a total hero isn't possible in today's society." In a special issue of Newsweek, a popular moviemaker reportedly said, "I believe that we are at a fairly frightening, transitional stage of history. We tried the Ozzie-and-Harriet thing in the 50s, and that didn't work. Then we tried the hippie peace-and-love thing, and the world got worse. So what's next? Today, there is no clear way for us to go. All we have are politicians, TV preachers, and cynical heavy-metal musicians telling us things that we sense are lies. No one is offering . . . the truth."[ii]

We wholeheartedly disagree. Beyond the counterfeits and media-hyped imitations, there are worthy heroes to be found and followed. We can take courage from those heroes. Some are very close to home. A young man from Canada said, "Nothing gives me more courage to stand up to the pressures around me like knowing my friend is doing it, too. I say to myself, 'If he can do it, then I can do it too.'" Other worthy examples might include a helpful boss, a supportive spouse, or an understanding religious leader.

When we, as parents, find worthy examples and strive to emulate them, our children are better able to take courage from our examples. Amy, a seventeen-year-old from California said, "My parents are my heroes. Their example makes me want to do what's right." One young man, Reid, from Texas also found a hero in his father. This seventeen-year-old wrote, "My dad told me that he had never touched a cigarette in his whole life, and if I were to decide to try smoking, he wanted me to invite him, and he would smoke for the first time, too. Because of that, I still have never touched a cigarette, and I never will."

Like the characters in *The Wizard of Oz*, if we can learn to think our problems through, to gain heart by expressing emotion, and to find courage through the lives of worthy heroes, we will be able to support our family down the road of life. When the road construction zones of unhealthy stress cause headaches in the lives of our family, we can show them a detour around the stress because we travelled down that road already and figured out how to manage our own stress effectively.

But wait! There is another character in the story we are forgetting— Toto, Dorothy's dog. Did you know the word *toto* in Latin means "total, complete, whole"?

It is not enough to use intellect alone when dealing with the pressures and stress that confront us. Heart by itself is also insufficient. Courage without thought and feeling could end up causing more problems than it helps to solve. The goal that should drive us through our lives is the wise and sensitive combination of all these elements. There are lots of lions and tigers and bears out there. There are lots of wicked witches, too. By thinking things through, appropriately expressing emotion, and finding courage, we can overcome them all.

In your own family journey, you might be thinking the same question Jerrick's family asked, "Are we there yet?" Is this road construction zone of unhealthy stress ever going to end? We never stop facing pressure and stress in our lives, but when that road construction comes, we must not forget to take the detour and learn from the Scarecrow, the Tin Man, the Lion, and as Dorothy says in the movie—"Toto, too." As we discover that detour, our family members can follow our example, and we will all get past the construction together.

[PRINCIPLES OF ACTION]

How can you teach your children by example to more effectively deal with pressure and stress? Here are some keys:

» **Get a Brain:** Examine yourself and determine how much stress you have in your life. How would more appropriate planning and the occasional break help decrease that stress?

» **Have a Heart:** How do you express your emotions? Is there a better way for you to communicate your emotions to family members?

» **Take Courage:** Who are some of your worthy heroes? How has learning about them helped you deal with your own pressures?

[ENDNOTES]

i. Victor Fleming, *The Wizard of Oz* (Warner Bros, 1939), Rereleased 1998, DVD.

ii. "The New Teens, What Makes Them Different, Who Are Their Heroes?" *Newsweek*, ed. Richard Smith (Summer/Fall 1990), Vol. CXV No. 27.

[SECRET #4]

OPEN WINDOWS OF OPPORTUNITY

"It's as if someone closed a door in my face," Brad's friend once told him. The friend had tried to get a job as a teacher. He even took vacation time from his other job to do his required student teaching. He had sacrificed time and money only to find out, along with hundreds of other applicants, that he had not been hired.

Years later, Brad met his friend again. He was happily established in a career in which he found great satisfaction. "What about your teaching aspirations?" Brad asked.

"I was crushed at the time," the friend said, "But, looking back, I can see that not getting that job was the best thing that ever happened to me." That closed door had forced him to search himself, stretch and develop, and find out where else he would be productive and happy.

One young woman, after waiting for her boyfriend to return from college, was disappointed to find he was no longer interested in her. She was hurt and angry, and her self-confidence was shaken. Later, after she was happily married to another young man, she ran into this particular ex-boyfriend again. It was clear from their discussion that the right decision had been made; they simply would not have been good for each other.

When Jerrick was a toddler, his dad, Rob, worked construction as a lather. He installed the metal or gypsum lath boards used to adhere stucco coatings to the sides of buildings. The work was difficult, especially in the summer heat, and the compensation was poor.

One day, Rob stayed late to clean up the construction site. As he was walking, he stepped on a thick metal strap used to transport lumber from the yard to the site. The strap flew up and sliced open his left eye. Rob's vision was lost immediately, but hundreds of stitches and months of lying flat on his back saved the eye itself. During that time, he lost his job as a lather and struggled to make ends meet financially.

Rob began to search for other avenues in which to use his construction expertise and support his family as he was recuperating. He studied for months, passed the general contractors exam, and started his own business building custom homes that has lasted for almost twenty years.

At times, all of us run into closed doors. They are rarely pleasant, seldom wanted, and never expected. However, when seen in a broader perspective, closed doors may actually be helpful to us as they lead us to open windows of even greater opportunities.

"It was as if someone closed a door in my face," Brad's friend had said. He was confused, wondering why his hard work to become a teacher hadn't produced the desired results. Yet, years later, he was grateful that the closed door had led him to his current success. Jerrick's dad had a similar experience. Due to injury, one door was closed, but that closed door led him to other opportunities.

When certain events in our lives appear to be setbacks that could negatively affect our family, and when hard work seems to go unrewarded, we can react positively. We can learn that secret and—instead of feeling discouraged and seeing setbacks as brick walls stretching on forever—ask ourselves two important questions: "What other options are open to me?" and "What would family members and friends advise me to do?" Then, when our children are faced with closed doors, we can stay positive and point them to open windows of opportunity because we've discovered those secret windows ourselves.

[WHAT OTHER OPTIONS ARE OPEN?]

With any action, an equal and opposite reaction must occur. It's simple physics. That means that each door slammed in our face causes something else to happen. Maybe that something was a ruffling curtain because of the wind that the door created. Could that curtain be hiding an open window? Possibly. But you never know until you look.

We should take the time to evaluate our situation properly before jumping to the conclusion that all is lost. Explore every option and examine every window behind each curtain. The closed door may lead us to a window, but there is the possibility of that window being locked. During those times, we shouldn't get discouraged. We should continue on until we find the open window we need.

During one summer, Jerrick needed to find a full-time job near his home because of a recent "collision" with a closed door. He applied for multiple positions, but none of them ended up being his open window. There was one particular job he was extremely interested in. After going through several separate interviews and job shadows with the company, he was turned down at the end of the interview process. Eventually, he took a promising job on the other side of the country. After a few weeks, however, the job didn't pan out, and he returned home, disheartened by the experience.

Finally, when he started to believe that he was destined for a jobless summer, he found a job with a concrete company. That job was the open window he was looking for, but it took a few locked windows before he found the one that was open. Jerrick can now share that experience with his future children and be an example to them as doors close in their faces and they struggle to find open windows.

Occasionally, we might find a few more open windows than we expected. We should still take the time to examine all our options before we make final decisions.

[WHAT WOULD FAMILY MEMBERS AND FRIENDS ADVISE?]

When closed doors force us to try and find open windows, we don't need to search alone. Family members and trusted friends are willing to help advise us where those open windows might be.

A woman was discouraged because she wanted to start a family of her own with a special someone in her life. The only problem was, she couldn't find that special someone. Door after door of eligible bachelors kept metaphorically closing in her face. When her thirtieth birthday approached, this woman decided she would finally accept the help of her family members who were constantly offering to line her up on blind dates—thirty of them to be exact. She made a deal with her family and friends that they could set her up with thirty different men in hopes that one of them might turn out to be her future husband.

Thirty dates later, the woman still hadn't found anyone. Then a family member set her up one last time. Number thirty-one turned out to be the one, and they were married soon after they met. It took trying thirty closed doors and locked windows to find an open one, but the open window wouldn't have been discovered without the help of family and friends.

Like this woman, it is important to remember that our family is here to help us. As parents, we might be determined to figure things out for ourselves and push away the help of our friends and relatives because we are used to giving advice, not taking it—but that isn't always the best solution. We should seek advice from our spouses, parents, and even our own children about how to find the open window.

Back in 1999, Jim Morris was a high school teacher and baseball coach in Texas. He was thirty-five years old, married, with three young children. His baseball team was good that year, but he was still struggling to motivate his players. Reagan County High School hadn't made the playoffs in years, but Jim Morris believed in his players' abilities. He told them, "Follow your dreams."

His players then asked their coach, "What about your dreams?"

The players knew that their coach used to play in the minor leagues, but Jim Morris injured himself and that door was closed in his face, abruptly. The players could see in their coach's eyes, however, that Jim Morris still had a dream to play major league baseball. They dared him that if the team made the playoffs, Jim would try out for a major league baseball team. Jim agreed.

A few months later, Jim found himself at a Tampa Bay Devil Rays' tryout session because he needed to make good on his deal. He waited for hours on end and, finally, was given the opportunity to step on to the mound and showcase his old, rusty skills. Twelve consecutive 98-mile-per-hour pitches later and Jim Morris was on his way to fulfilling his dream of playing in the major leagues. The high school baseball coach found that open window because he followed the advice of his own players, and the players found the will to win because they believed in their coach and saw him reaching toward his goals.[i]

In the same way, when we follow the advice given to us by our own spouse, parents, or children, we can find open windows in places where we might otherwise not have looked. Then our children will have extra confidence in following the advice we give them on where to look for open windows because they see us following others' advice and succeeding.

When Jim Morris drove that long road to the Tampa Bay Devil Rays' baseball tryouts, he probably thought, "Am I there yet?" Are we asking the same question in our journey toward family happiness? "Are we there yet? When will our dreams become reality?" Not yet. In fact, we may find that the road we were on was not even the right one because we just hit a dead end—a metaphorical door closed in the face of our journey—but wait! We found a secret. There's a dirt road to the side, an open window. We can shift the car into four-wheel drive by examining our options and seeking the advice of family members. The closed doors we encounter may lead us toward open windows of opportunity.

[PRINCIPLES OF ACTION]

How can you discover the open windows in your life? Here are some reminders:

» **What Options Are Open?:** Take time to examine every opportunity available to you. How can you look at the positives and negatives of each?

» **What Would Family Members and Friends Advise?:** Think of a time when you took advice from a family member or friend. How did that advice help you?

[ENDNOTES]

i. Plaschke, Bill. "Living the Impossible Dream." *Los Angeles Times*, 21 September 1999.

GET OVER BEING UNDERAPPRECIATED

A mother fixes dinner for hungry family members who eat and then disappear without offering a kind word or help with the dishes. A father returns from a long business trip, and his teenage daughter welcomes him home by asking for money. An aunt and uncle plan the family reunion only to be told that it wasn't as good as last year. Certainly there is no shortage of people who have experienced the discouragement and frustration of feeling underappreciated. "This is a nice Christmas tree, but where are the lights?" "This is a nice casserole, but where is dessert?" "This is a nice visit, but where is the rest of your family?"

At one time or another, each of us feels the sting of being under-appreciated—especially parents. In these moments, it is important to learn the secrets that can help us get over that sting. We can learn to cultivate magnanimity and choose happiness.

[CULTIVATE MAGNANIMITY]

To be magnanimous means to be noble and generous in forgiving. It describes a person who strives to be free of petty feelings and chooses to act. The word comes from Latin roots: *magnus*, meaning "great," and *animus*, which means "spirit." A magnanimous person, then, shows a great spirit by acting positively toward people and circumstances rather than reacting negatively to them.

One woman prepares a flower arrangement for a community meeting each week. It is not her responsibility; she just does it because she hopes it will make others feel welcome and comfortable. A family chooses another family less fortunate than theirs every Christmas and gives gifts to that chosen family anonymously. Each month, a barber takes his supplies to a local park and gives haircuts to the homeless free of charge. A widow and her grandson repair broken books they gather from garage sales and thrift stores and donate them to libraries and schools. No one beyond their family is even aware of their private efforts.

Jerrick's family was once struggling through financial difficulties. A construction accident disabled his dad for several months when Jerrick was a young boy. During that time, what little money the family had saved up was quickly spent. An unknown individual placed some money on their doorstep without a note or any way to contact him or her. Although it wasn't an extremely large amount of money, to Jerrick's family it felt like ten thousand dollars. His family wished they could thank the responsible people, but they never found out who placed that money on their doorstep. These are examples of magnanimity.

None of the magnanimous people described searched out recognition for their efforts. They served others because they wanted to. When we give selfless acts of service to others, we forget our own situations for a time. When we reflect back on our own lives after serving others, we find a renewed focus on the things that really matter rather than dwelling on the small distractions.

Life gets hectic, and often we, as parents, can feel underappreciated for our service to our family, but we don't have to feel that way. Parenting itself is a magnanimous action. Think about it—who in his or her right mind would willingly take on trying to balance one child's dance practice, another's football practice, a sick child, and a screaming baby while at the same time accommodating a spouse's needs? Parenting is the ultimate magnanimous action because we willingly chose to act and create a family, taking on all the joys and challenges that come with that undertaking. When we view parenting as the magnanimous undertaking that it is, we can then choose to act and create our own happiness rather than reacting to the actions of our family members and letting those actions determine our happiness.

[CHOOSE HAPPINESS]

On Brad's kitchen wall hangs a plaque that reads, "Happiness is a city in the state of mind." He keeps it there to remind himself that we are in charge of our own attitudes. If you are having a bad day, others aren't really to blame, even when you feel underappreciated.

We are responsible for our own actions. In the same way, we are responsible for our own attitudes and our own happiness. No one can choose what we're thinking or feeling for us. We can have a good attitude toward whatever situation we happen to be in.

If we let our happiness rest on the actions and moods of others, we will always be disappointed. If our happiness is dependent on perfect situations, it will always be a future dream, forever out of reach. Happiness depends not on what others do for us, but on what we do for others and the inner peace we feel from that service. Happiness doesn't depend on thank-you cards or public praise. Our happiness is completely within our own control.

Some may be thinking, "But wait, I can't be happy until I get a job," or "Once I move out of this place, I can be happy." Although getting a new job may be necessary, and moving certainly can bring a change in our lives, our overall happiness is still within our control—job or no job, change or no change.

People who are always waiting for the next big event to happen in their lives to make them happy—such as getting a promotion, paying off the house, retiring, or graduating—will never be truly happy. They will be stuck in a perpetual rat race, always looking ahead to the next milestone until there's none left to accomplish. It's much better to find joy in the journey toward each milestone.

Consider a parent who makes a nice dinner for his or her children. He or she might make the dinner with an end goal in mind, possibly a goal of getting a thank you. If that thank you doesn't come, the parent would feel underappreciated and disappointed. On the other hand, if someone finds joy in serving by making the dinner, although it still might sting to not receive a thank you, the sting is lessened by the joy that person found making the dinner itself. He or she can then decide to be happy, regardless of the end result. That parent is in the best frame of mind to teach children to be more appreciative rather than demanding gratitude.

Happy people aren't happy solely because of their accomplishments in life. Many people have accomplished much and still aren't happy. Happy people aren't happy because of the praise and appreciation they receive from others. Some people receive a lot of loving praise and still aren't happy. Happy people are happy because they find joy in the moment. They can separate an end result from the steps it takes to get there, and they find joy in the journey. A hike is beautiful, not just because of the view from the summit, but because of the experiences all along the way. The same can be said for our lives with our family.

At this point, we're still asking the same question as Jerrick's family: "Are we there yet?" Not quite. For parents, the journey will always be long. The road is especially difficult when we feel like our attempts to make the ride as comfortable as possible for our family are unappreciated. A few sincere expressions of gratitude can make a big difference, but whether or not they come, the secret is cultivating magnanimity and choosing happiness throughout the journey of life.

[PRINCIPLES OF ACTION]

How can you avoid dwelling on feeling underappreciated? Here are some ideas to consider:

> » **Cultivate Magnanimity:** People can either choose to act toward a situation or react because of a situation. When have you chosen to act or react, and why?
> » **Choose Happiness:** Do you sometimes allow the actions of others to determine your happiness? In what ways can you determine your own happiness more often?

[SECRET #6]

MAKE HONESTY YOUR *ONLY* POLICY

"Please don't tell my parents," a young girl tearfully pleaded with the director of the summer youth program she was attending. She had just been caught shoplifting several hundred dollars' worth of merchandise from the college campus bookstore.

A young man came to his youth program director privately to say that his roommate had marijuana in their dorm room. When the director approached the roommate, the young man lied, saying he knew nothing about the illegal drug. Then, when the police produced evidence, he changed his story: "It was there when I checked into the room. I was going to tell you—honestly, I promise."

In a recent *New York Times* article, it was reported that "a majority of students violate standards of academic integrity to some degree" and there is "evidence that the problem has worsened over the last few decades."[i] Cheating isn't limited to struggling students. Students at the top of their class are just as likely to cheat as students at the bottom.

Recently, Jerrick was speaking with two students who had just finished taking an exam. The exam was open book (the two words college students love to hear, along with "class cancelled"). In fact, the only rule given by the professor was that students could not collaborate with other students on the exam. Regardless of the rule, one of the students Jerrick talked to had observed three of her classmates gathered together with their laptops. Sure enough, these three students were taking the test together to save time.

Shoplifting, lying, cheating—people usually resort to such dishonest behavior for four main reasons: (1) to gain immediate satisfaction without having to wait or work for it, (2) to conceal guilt and avoid unpleasant consequences, (3) to impress others and win acceptance or approval, or (4) to avoid ridicule or embarrassment.

Young people often do not understand that rules such as "Shoplifters will be prosecuted," "If you are caught cheating you will fail the assignment," and the common parental rule "Tell the truth," are given not just out of concern for the property and rights of others, but out of concern for them.

The secret parents need to learn and communicate to their children is that those who engage in dishonest behavior lose the respect and trust of people around them and, worse, begin to doubt themselves and to distrust others.

A movie called *The Mountain* tells the story of two brothers who arrived at the site of an airplane crash in the Alps and found a single survivor. One occupied himself with preparing a makeshift sled to transport the injured survivor down the mountain. The other brother spent his time stealing money and valuables belonging to crash victims. Then, when he noticed that his brother had crossed the chasm between the crash site and the path to the nearest town, the thief demanded to know how he could safely cross the chasm. His brother knew that the ice bridge spanning the deep ravine was unstable, so he warned the thief not to cross that way. But the thief, judging his brother to be as dishonest as he was, chose to cross by the unsafe bridge—and died when it collapsed into the gorge.[ii]

Dishonest people who judge the sincere words and actions of others as a hoax, a "show," or a manipulation may endanger themselves by ignoring honesty when it comes.

What can we do to create a pattern of honesty in our homes? Here are some secrets to keep in mind.

[SET A GOOD EXAMPLE]

Do our family members hear us lie occasionally to cover our errors? Do we say "I tried to call you" instead of "I meant to call you"? Do they see us copying DVDs or streaming music that carries copyright restrictions? Whatever example we set, we can expect it to stay in our family members' minds.

One young mother recalls a visit to the dentist when she was a teen growing up in a small farming community. After the dentist had finished his work, she told him, "If you will put that on my father's bill, he will pay you later."

"I know," the dentist replied. "He always does. Your father is a very, very honest man." She already knew that her father was a fine man, but it made a deep impression on her to realize that others recognized and depended on his honesty. "I've always tried to live so that people could say that about me, too," she reflects.

[CARE]

Often, our children and other family members do not need instruction on honesty as much as they need motivation. They need to feel a personal desire to incorporate honesty into their lives. One of the best motivations we can offer in this regard is a strong emotional bond with our family members.

Some children look at adults as obstacles to get around, but children will never want to hurt or disappoint parents who openly express love, concern, and trust. One friend told us that when others would invite him to participate in questionable activities while he was growing up, he would always say no. "It wasn't because of the punishment I might receive if I were caught, but because I knew how much my dad loved me, and how disappointed he would be if I ever broke his confidence."

[GIVE THEM A SAY]

Unrealistic expectations, habitual nagging, or long lists of "musts," "don'ts," and "can'ts" often leave young people feeling helplessly fenced in. For some, dishonesty becomes their way of fighting back—taking control where no control is allowed.

Of course, we all have freedom to make choices, and regardless of the situation, the responsibility for a dishonest choice rests on the shoulders of the individual making it. Unfortunately, some family members may resort to dishonest behavior simply to "survive" or to handle an overbearing environment in which they feel they have little control or will not be listened to or understood.

Parents can recognize that children are in the process of developing their ability to make choices about their lives. Like all of us, they need to feel that they have a say in what happens to them. While parents may need to establish reasonable guidelines, we should allow them to make their own choices about some things as soon as they are able.

[PRAISE HONESTY]

When your children admit to a minor wrongdoing or take responsibility for their own embarrassing behavior, make a point to tell them how good it is that they are being honest.

As Brad and his brothers grew up, his mother sometimes asked questions like "Who ate the chocolate chips I've been saving?" When Brad was brave enough to admit that he had downed the whole package himself, he knew there was a mini lecture on nutrition in store. But he also knew that his mom would say, "I appreciate your honesty." That was the phrase he could always count on hearing. Then she would continue: "I'm glad to know that you admit it when you do something wrong, because now, when you say you didn't do something, I'll trust you."

When you observe someone being honest, point it out to your children. A widow living on a very small income found a mechanic she trusted to make needed repairs on her car. Sometimes she could have had the work done for less by taking the car to another shop, but she always told her son that she knew Mr. Mitchell would not recommend work that didn't need to be done or charge her more than necessary. Her son learned two things: where to take his own car when it needed repairs and how to conduct his own business so that others would have similar confidence in his work.

[MAINTAIN ACCOUNTABILITY]

A young woman admitted to her teacher that she had plagiarized a paper. The teacher thanked her for her honesty but explained that her grade would still have to be lowered and that the work would have to be redone. The girl was upset. She had been "let off the hook" in the past for telling the truth, and she had come to look upon honesty as just another strategy to avoid natural consequences.

It's true that Brad's mother used to tell him she appreciated his honesty for admitting that he had eaten the chocolate chips she was saving. But Brad was then expected to go to the store, buy a new package of chocolate chips, and help her make the cookies she needed for her meeting.

If we, as parents, do not require that broken windows be replaced and stolen merchandise paid for, we, too, are stealing—robbing our children of a vital and important part of their needed attempts at restitution.

When several young men arrived late to a school dance, the chaperone smelled alcohol on their breath. These young men knew that they were breaking school rules. The boys were well known and well liked, so the other young people at the dance watched carefully to see what would happen.

The chaperone kindly asked them to leave and escorted them out of the building. Because they were in no condition to drive, another chaperone who knew the young men well volunteered to take them home.

The young men protested, saying they were sorry, they hadn't drunk all that much, and they would never do it again. But when their words had no effect on the chaperon's decision to send them home to their parents, they became angry. The chaperone who knew the young men calmly reminded them that they were the ones who had chosen this consequence; if they should be angry at anyone, it was themselves. His actions showed how much he really cared—enough to risk his good relationship with them by standing firmly against what they had done.

[CORRECT IN PRIVATE]

When problems occur, it's best to deal with guilty family members in private rather than before others. Seek a quiet time—right before bed, for example. In planning what to say, think of yourself as a consultant rather than a manager. Think of the conversation as an exploration rather than an accusation. Start by asking "What happened?" or

"What's wrong?" instead of "I know you've been lying to me, and I want to know why."

Your children may say, "There's nothing wrong." Such a response may only be a test to see if you really care enough to ask again. Don't give up. Keep the conversation going or wait in silence. If you are still met with a blank stare or a "wasn't me," you can decide whether to present the facts you are aware of or to simply leave your son or daughter to think alone and pick the conversation up again later.

Once the dishonesty is admitted—when your child or other family member realizes that his or her actions were unjustified and wrong—help him or her come up with a positive plan of action for the future and commit to it. Express your love and your confidence in his or her desires and ability to make things right and make better choices in the future.

[DISHONESTY IS A SYMPTOM]

If dishonest behavior continues to surface, be careful not to overreact. Statements such as "I thought we'd been through all this before," "You're nothing but a thief," or "I'm ashamed to be your father" will only make the situation worse.

Rarely is dishonesty the root problem. Lying, cheating, stealing, and vandalism are usually symptoms of other difficulties—possibly low self-esteem, poor communication skills, or an inability to cope with stress and pressure.

The best way to address dishonest behavior is to focus on those underlying problems. Many of those problems are covered in this book. Chapter ten addresses low self-esteem, chapters thirteen and fourteen discuss important communication skills, and chapter three talks about dealing with pressures and stress. Professional counseling is an avenue that's also available if the problems persist.

[NEVER GIVE UP]

Sometimes we try diligently to do all of the things suggested above, and still family members elect to be dishonest. We must never forget that we cannot control another's actions. Each individual makes choices, and when a person chooses to do something wrong, he or she must accept responsibility. People often rationalize it, justifying their actions or pretending they "didn't know." But they must learn that we are all accountable for our own actions. We must not shield our children from natural consequences, but we also should never give up trying to teach and persuade others in love.

"Are we there yet?" No, but honesty helps in our journey to family happiness. Honesty is like following the laws of the road during our journey; honesty makes family life safe and bearable. When we help our children and other family members develop a pattern of honesty in their lives, they will be able to experience for themselves the peace and joy that being honest can bring. Wise people realize that honesty is not just the best policy. It is the *only* policy.

[PRINCIPLES OF ACTION]

How can you establish honesty within your home? Here are some points that must not be overlooked:

» **Set a Good Example:** Take a moment to examine your own life. In what ways could you be more honest with yourself and with others?

» **Care:** When family members know you care about them, they are less likely to be dishonest. In what ways do you show family members that you care?

» **Give Them a Say:** Family members, especially teenagers, need opportunities to make many of their own decisions. How does allowing family members to make their own choices establish a pattern of trust, honesty, and accountability in their lives?

» **Praise Honesty, but Maintain Accountability:** Look back on the past week. How are you recognizing and appreciating honest behavior? Have you maintained accountability when a family member broke a rule? What happened when you required accountability or didn't?

» **Dishonesty Is a Symptom, so Never Give Up:** What underlying causes can you see for why a family member chooses to be dishonest? How can you address those causes? You can't force dishonest family members to become honest. It is their choice, but never give up on them! We can all learn and make positive changes.

[ENDNOTES]

i. Richard Perez-Pena, "Studies Find More Students Cheating, With High Achievers No Exception," *New York Times*, 7 Sept. 2012.

ii. Edward Dmytryk, *The Mountain* (Paramount Pictures, 1956), based on the novel by Henri Troyat, VHS.

[SECRET #7]

WATCH OVER THE WEB

Most people recognize that staying in contact with family and good friends by e-mail and through social networking sites is a wonderful benefit of the Internet. As an educational resource and source of information, the Internet is extremely useful, providing everything from directions to a destination, to the current time in a foreign country, to the availability of tickets for an upcoming show.

But most also acknowledge Internet drawbacks and dangers, including pornography. A young man admitted, "I became addicted to porn because it was so easily available on the Internet. Each time I viewed it, I wanted pictures that were more graphic and extreme. It became a huge problem for me before I finally had the courage to talk with my parents and start trying to break the habit. I'd give anything to have never gotten involved in the first place."

Chat rooms can also be very dangerous. One young woman said, "I read about a thirteen-year-old girl who was getting a lot of attention from guys she met on the Internet and ended up arranging meetings with them. She was murdered by one of them. That really scared me."

Gambling and online games are also cyber-dangers. One teenager explained, "Many games are full of violence, but the biggest problem is that they're just a big waste of time."

How can we help family members take advantage of the Internet's benefits and avoid its pitfalls? Many adults believe it is as easy as installing protection programs and passwords, but some youth have pointed out that such software is no cure-all. One young man said, "If parents think their children are safe just because they bought some program, they'd better think again. There are lots of ways around the programs, and you can always find a computer or hand-held device someplace that doesn't have any safeguards. Besides, even if the software blocks what kids have access to, it doesn't keep them safe from predators."

A young woman related, "There's really no safety program that is totally safe. If you want to do bad things on the Internet, you'll find a way. Parents have to focus on other ways to protect kids as well." The secret is to supplement software protection by teaching family members to use the Internet wisely.

[KEEP COMPUTERS IN HIGH-TRAFFIC AREAS]

Do not allow computers, laptops, or tablets to be used in bedrooms. Put them in the family room, office, or dining area. Keep the screen of the computer facing the center of the room and not a wall. One teenager said, "My mom moved our computer right into the dining area by the phone where everyone is passing by all the time." Another said, "My parents have our computer in my dad's study, but they installed doors with windows so they can easily see what's on the screen, even if the door is closed to keep the dog out."

[LIMIT SCREEN TIME]

It is obvious that the more time people spend online, the more likely they are to engage in inappropriate activities. One teen explained, "My parents put a time limit on screen time. By the time I do my homework and check Facebook, I don't have any time left to look for trouble."

One might think teens would rebel at such restraints. On the contrary, many teens are grateful for them. One said, "This way I have more time in my life for other things, and I feel like a better person because of it." However, if teenagers don't see their parents making the same efforts to limit their screen time, teenagers will be more likely to rebel against those constraints. As parents, we need to make sure we follow our own advice and not let screen time cut into family time.

[ENCOURAGE OTHER INTERESTS AND ACTIVITIES]

"I spent way too much time on the computer and was getting into some stuff I shouldn't have," said one young man. "Then my dad helped me buy and start fixing up a 1984 Toyota Tercel, and I didn't care much about the computer anymore." Of course, buying a car is not the answer for every child, but shifting a young person's focus toward a variety of interests is healthy. Another boy said, "My parents keep me busy, so I don't have free time to surf the Web." A young woman mentioned involvement in other personal and family activities: "My parents encourage me to read instead of watch TV and play on the Internet. They also read to us as a family. Believe it or not, those types of activities really do help."

[CHECK COMPUTER AND DATA RECORDS]

"Some people call it snooping, but my mom just calls it 'good, old-fashioned parenting,'" one girl said of her parents' practice of keeping track of what she does online or with her smart phone. We should learn how to check the history of what sites have been visited (yes, that can be done on a smart phone or tablet), and don't be afraid to talk to family members about anything that seems questionable. One young woman said, "My parents usually let us use the computer only when they are home, but they also go through the files to see where we've been. That's how my brother got caught looking at pornography, and Mom and Dad were able to start helping him." Some parents woudn't dream of letting kids go out with strangers, but they don't even ask about Internet activity or check on their own kids' Facebook pages or Twitter feeds. As parents appropriately monitor their children's technology use, they are better able to guide and teach their children.

[DISCOURAGE UNSUPERVISED SLEEPOVERS]

"Nothing very good ever happens at sleepovers, even when you are with good kids," one young man said. "I'm not talking about Scout camp where adults are around. I'm talking about just kicking it with your buddies. It gets late and guys start talking, and pretty soon you're on the computer or phones. It just leads to trouble." Too many people have made poor choices at sleepovers when they were younger. That's often when they have first let down their guards and have gotten involved with drinking, pornography, sexual experimentation, sexual abuse, and vandalism.

[POST UPLIFTING PICTURES BY THE COMPUTER OR AS PHONE BACKGROUNDS]

"Having a picture of a role model next to the computer helps me remember how much I want to make right choices and be like him," said one young woman. One young man admitted, "I have been tempted many times to view filth on the Internet, but my mom has pictures of my little nephews right next to the screen. It reminds me of my responsibility to be a role model for them. How can I view filth and feel good about myself? How can I view things I wouldn't want them to see?"

The background of Jerrick's phone is a picture of his family. Every time he turns it on, he sees that picture, and it provides the same motivation for him that the picture of the little nephews provided for that young man. How can he use his phone capabilities to engage in harmful activities while knowing that he needs to be an example for his family?

[TALK ABOUT INTERNET USE]

Nothing is more helpful than parents asking questions and speaking openly about Internet dangers with children. One young man reported, "The thing that helps me most is being able to talk with my parents. My dad told me how pornography can mess up my life and ruin my future marriage. He says pornography weakens the trust, love, and commitment that are essential for a healthy sexual relationship in marriage. Someday, when I'm married, I want my wife to be able to trust me." Another said, "Even when I slip up, I can talk to my dad and know he won't blow up. He doesn't make me feel like slime. He just helps me try to be better."

Teens are grateful when parents don't just make a rule, but also explain why it's a rule. A young woman said, "My parents talk to me about the pros and cons of spending time on Facebook. Discussing it openly helps me make better choices."

[SEEK COMMITMENTS]

It is helpful when parents approach children in private and ask point-blank questions about Internet use. Parents who ask for private promises about what will or will not be done on the Internet or with smart phones have the greatest success. One young man explained, "My parents used to have a screening system, but it was really messing things up because it would block sites that shouldn't have been blocked. It wouldn't even let us look up sites we needed for homework, so we finally removed it. That's when my parents told me that the best filter is my conscience. They put the responsibility on me and asked me to commit to staying clear of dangerous stuff. That helped me a lot." A young woman related, "My parents asked me to promise them I wouldn't go into chat rooms. They trust me, and I don't want to lose that trust." Another young man recounted, "When I left for college this past year, my parents asked me to promise them I would make smart decisions when I got to the dorms and had access to computers without safety programs. That promise has been the best safety program ever."

"Are we there yet?" Not yet. No doubt the Internet is like a useful map that can help us along the way, but it can also lead to detours that will delay us in our journey and distract us from reaching our ultimate destination. When children get old enough to drive, one of the first things they're taught is to keep their eyes on the road and avoid distractions. With Internet use, the secret is that there is much we can do beyond simply installing protection software. Parents can make a positive difference in the never-ending fight against negative influences on the Internet by teaching their children to keep their eyes on the road and avoid the harmful distractions of the Internet.

[PRINCIPLES OF ACTION]

How can you monitor your family's computer use? Here are some suggestions:

» **Keep Computers in High Traffic Areas:** What are some benefits of keeping computers in more public areas of your house? What are options for your family if people aren't always home at the same time?

» **Limit Screen Time and Encourage Other Activities:** How would limiting the time you spend on social networking sites help you to be more productive throughout the day? What are other beneficial hobbies that you or other family members could pursue during the time you devote to the computer?

» **Check Computer and Data Records:** Do you know how to check what your children are doing on the computer or on their phones? Who could help you find out?

» **Post Uplifting Pictures:** What picture is set as the background of your computer or phone, and does it provide positive motivation for you to make right choices with technology?

» **Talk about Internet Use and Seek Commitments:** How do you discuss the house rules about Internet usage with your family members? When you make a commitment to someone else, how does being accountable to that person give you motivation to keep that commitment? How often should you revisit those conversations?

[SECRET #8]

KEEP A JOURNAL

With everything else parents have to do in a day, why journals? We tell ourselves, "Journals are for posterity," and then think, "Well, maybe my grandson will break both legs and be desperate enough for something to do that he'll pull out my dust-covered journal." But the remote possibility of such an event in the future never provides much motivation. The secret is that writing in a journal is valuable for us in its own right—whether our grandchildren ever read it or not.

Writing is an important form of communication, but that is scarcely its major value. Like shooting baskets all alone in your driveway, writing does not require an audience beyond yourself to be worthwhile or enjoyable.

When Brad's in-laws were moving to Colorado, a tragic moving-van fire destroyed all their belongings, including family photograph albums and personal journals. One well-meaning friend lamented, "All that work for nothing!"

Brad's wise mother-in-law responded, "The process we went through writing our journals can never be burned. Every hour we spent on those books helped to make us the people we have become."

Like Brad's mother-in-law, we can find personal journals to be an ideal environment in which to "become" the people we want to become.

Whether handwritten or electronic, a journal is a perfect place for us to think, feel, discover, expand, remember, and dream.

[THINK]

A student once asked a college professor what he thought about a particular issue. He said, "I don't know. I've never written anything about it." His response was puzzling to the student initially, but not once the student reflected on the answer.

"Thoughts are created in the act of writing. [It is a myth that] you must have something to say in order to write. [In reality,] you often need to write in order to have anything to say. Thought comes with writing, and writing may never come if it is postponed until we are satisfied that we have something to say. . . . The assertion of write first, see what you had to say later applies to all manifestations of written language, to letters . . . as well as to diaries and journals."[i]

Simple journal activities can get our thoughts flowing and add perspective to our family relationships. Do you ever have days when you feel ignored by your family members? Try venting in your journal that night and writing about the things that made you feel appreciated that day or the things that made you happy that day. It will brighten up your outlook and help you to dwell on the positive. Depression might be offset by making a list of the things you were grateful for that day, and feeling overwhelmed can be remedied by a thoughtful entry about the little things your children and family members have done to help you throughout the day. Whatever you do, remember that journal writing is personal and free-flowing—follow your thoughts and experiment with them to make your life more fulfilling.

[FEEL]

Journal writing reinforces the idea that each person is important. As parents, sometimes we can feel like the little things we do for our family members each day are unimportant or don't really matter in the long run. However, our experiences—even the small, every day experiences—and feelings are valuable and are worth recording so they are not lost. In addition to validating feelings, journals provide a safe place to express them. Journal writing puts us in the difficult but valuable position of finding words for hard-to-express ideas and feelings. The effort we put forth verbalizing our thoughts and feelings helps us come to know ourselves better.

Jerrick remembers a time when he had to have a difficult conversation with a person he cared about very much. He didn't want to hurt this person's feelings, so he wrote his ideas on paper first. This helped him better understand his own thoughts and feelings because he had to explain his feelings to himself before he explained them to his friend.

When the conversation happened, Jerrick was better able to communicate his thoughts and feelings in a respectful way. Both individuals involved in the conversation came away with a better understanding of each other. Even though Jerrick didn't bring his journal entry with him, the act of writing his feelings down helped him remember what he wanted to say during the critical conversation and how to phrase it in such a way that it wouldn't hurt the other person's feelings.

[DISCOVER]

It is said that later in Helen Keller's life, when she would do presentations and field questions, the audiences would compliment her on her writing and ask how she decided what to write about. She would say that although she spoke through an interpreter, she didn't want to live in a hand-me-down world of others' experiences. She always preferred to write about her own feelings, fears, and discoveries.

A popular country song expresses the same feeling: "I want to talk about me." Often, we may want to talk about "me," but don't want to monopolize a conversation or seem disinterested in other people involved in the conversation. With journal writing, you can talk about you—your hopes, dreams, and wishes—without feeling guilty about not listening to other people.

Often, simply by writing about ourselves we begin to see life from a new perspective. A young woman put it this way: "My journal gives me a chance to discover things about myself I didn't even know were there. As I write, I can figure out who I really am."

[EXPAND]

Journals invite us to record what we do each day. If we expect ourselves to write about experiences, we will seek out more meaningful experiences in our lives.

Writing, like other arts, is a representation of life. Thus, the writer is compelled to live life more consciously. Journal writing will not make passive people miraculously more active. However, regular writing does make it harder for us to remain passive.

Some people feel like they don't have anything to write about. They perceive their lives as boring, simple, or mundane. The sometimes-monotonous job of parenthood might not seem journal worthy. Even if you think there's nothing of value in your day, write about it anyway. You'll often surprise yourself as you discover how the simple things in life expand to take on new meaning as you reflect on them.

Courtney and Addam Roberts, Jerrick's sister and brother-in-law, recently became new parents to an adorable little girl named Brynley. Once she was born, Courtney and Addam realized that they didn't want to forget this newborn stage of their daughter's life. They video her often and write about the funny sounds she makes and the funny things she does every day. Even though many of these things could be considered normal activities for babies, such as rolling over or falling asleep in interesting positions, Courtney and Addam find that they appreciate those little things more as they reflect on how quickly Brynley is growing up.

Journals don't just help us expand and seek out new experiences, they also help us expand and find new joy in the everyday experiences we are already having.

[REMEMBER]

Writing down experiences can help us remember them longer and with greater accuracy. Journals make it easy to look back over our lives and see the progress we are—or are not—making. They can motivate us to stay on course or make positive changes.

When Jerrick and his wife, Aimee, fist started dating, they sat down and tried to chart their relationship: where they met, what sorts of activities they did together, movies they'd watched, and discussions they'd had. Even though they had only known each other for a few months at the time, they found that—even with both minds working together—it was very difficult to remember those activities and the order in which they occurred. Aimee commented, "It sure would be easier if we had our journals!" As usual, she was right.

Of course, some memories we may wish to forget. Even though it may hurt to write down those experiences, and even though you may want to tear those pages out, try not to. You never know what you may learn from them in the future. In the meantime, you can take those unpleasant memories off the front burner of your brain knowing that they are now stored in your journal.

[DREAM]

"Journal writing . . . [provides] a place for self-expression where one can afford to take a risk, experiment with ideas and materials, and even make a mistake."[ii] Because a journal is unstructured, many find it instantly inviting—it's a protected place, an invitation to open up.

As with backdoor friends who have never seen our best china, the pages of our journal invite us to share ourselves—our real selves. They are a safe place for our most personal goals and deepest dreams.

On Saturday, June 20, 1942, Anne Frank, a young Jewish girl who eventually died in the Holocaust, wrote the following in her personal journal: "I haven't written for a few days, because I wanted first of all to think about my diary. It's an odd idea for someone like me to keep a diary; not only because I have never done so before, but because it seems to me that neither I—nor, for that matter, anyone else—will be interested in the unbosomings of a thirteen-year-old school girl. Still, what does that matter? I want to write, but more than that, I want to bring out all kinds of things that lie buried deep in my heart."[iii]

As our personal journals become places where we can think, feel, discover, expand, remember, and dream, we will come to better understand ourselves and who we are becoming. In this digital age, pen and paper aren't the only way to keep a personal journal. Brad's journal is a notebook, but Jerrick's journal is in the form of a word document that he adds to weekly. Many people find word documents, private blogs, saved emails, and video journals to be just as effective as paper journals. Family members must find a journal format that's right for them. As we seek to record our dreams, aspirations, goals, triumphs, and lessons learned from failures, we'll either begin to feel comfortable with the mode we've chosen or we can try another method. The main thing is to just begin. If you use a digital journal, be sure to keep a backup of it somewhere.

"Are we there yet?" Not yet. In fact, our journey is very long and filled with many experiences—both good and bad, unique happenings and daily occurrences—but all are worth remembering. The secret is that keeping a journal will help us remember the memories we are creating on our family journey and will help make the journey more meaningful and fulfilling. In whatever form a journal takes, the time we spend keeping it is not wasted because it helps us become better as we continue toward our destination—whether our grandchildren ever read it or not.

[PRINCIPLES OF ACTION]

Despite busy schedules, how can you recognize the importance of keeping a journal? Here are some key points to consider:

> **Think and Feel:** A journal provides a private place for you to write down your thoughts and describe your feelings. How would writing down your daily thoughts help you? Why is it important to be able to write down what you're feeling?

> **Discover:** In what ways has writing in a journal allowed you to discover more about yourself?

> **Expand:** When you expect to write in your journal about your day, do you notice or seek out experiences to write about? How has that expanded your activities each day?

> **Remember:** Writing in a journal helps you remember experiences you would otherwise forget. Why would preserving those

memories help you later in life?

» **Dream:** Journal writing gives you a place to talk about your dreams and aspirations in life. How would writing about your goals help you along your path to accomplishing those goals?

[ENDNOTES]

i. Frank Smith, "Myths of Writing," *Language Arts* (1981), 58.7: 793, 795.

ii. M. Joan Lickteig, "Research-Based Recommendations for Teachers of Writing," *Language Arts* (1981), 58.1: 46.

iii. Anne Frank, *The Diary of a Young Girl*, Trans. B. M. Mooyaart (New York: Bantam, 1993).

[SECRET #9]

SHARE THE LOAD

W hen constructing a home, there's plenty of cleaning that needs to be done. Before a new phase of construction starts, the finished phase needs to be cleaned up. Imagine trying to carpet a house with sawdust on the floor! It just doesn't work. Even after a home is built, immense cleaning needs to happen before the homeowners can move in.

Unfortunately, the cleaning doesn't stop there! We live in our houses; they aren't showrooms (as much as many of us would like them to be, most often that isn't the case). Houses get dirty; kids run through the family room with muddy shoes, and endless cups get left on the countertop. Floors still need to be vacuumed, bathrooms cleaned, and yards maintained. If one person were to take on that challenge for an entire family, it would be intimidating to say the least. The secret is to share the load, first by learning how to divide work fairly between each spouse and then splitting it between the children, too. Luckily, there's work enough for everyone!

[THE BATHROOM DILEMMA]

"How do I get my wife to clean the bathroom?" The young man asking the question had been married only a few months. The realities and responsibilities of married life were beginning to sink in, and he had come to Brad with his concerns.

"Who says cleaning the bathroom is her job?" Brad asked.

The young man seemed startled. "Well, my sisters always did it, and I just thought . . . "

Brad said, "I grew up in a family of all boys. Who do you think cleaned the bathrooms in my house?"

This newlywed friend seemed amazed. But when Brad was growing up, his dad made it clear early on that there was no such thing as men's work or women's work. "There is just work that needs to be done, and we do it together," he would say.

Once we mentally accept a job as ours, we're in the right frame of mind to ask for—and appreciate—needed help.

As many married couples have learned, there is a big difference between "Please come and help me clean the bathroom" and "It's your job to clean the bathroom."

In marriage, a question could be asked: Why worry so much about what you feel your spouse should be doing when you should be more concerned about what you are doing—or aren't doing? In any relationship, the fruits of service are sweeter than the fruits of criticism.

Brad's young married friend thanked him for the advice and said good-bye. Brad didn't see him again for a while, but Brad knew he was doing just fine the day he ran into this young man's wife.

"So how's married life?" Brad asked her.

"Just wonderful," she replied, smiling broadly. "I'm married to the greatest husband on earth."

"Really? Does he clean bathrooms?" Brad prodded.

"Believe it or not, he does," she responded. "In fact, his motto is that there is no such thing as men's work or women's work. There's just work that needs to be done, and we do it together. Isn't that great?"

"It sure is," Brad said with a smile.

[WORKING TOGETHER]

Jerrick has an aunt named Brenda who's exactly a year older than his dad, Rob. A running joke in the family is that Rob always does the dishes when his sister Brenda drops in for an unexpected visit, creating the illusion that he always does the dishes. What Aunt Brenda doesn't know is that, when she's not around, her brother usually delegates that responsibility to his children. Sometimes they can still get their dad to come help them by teasing, "Is that Aunt Brenda we see coming up toward the house?"

All kidding aside, delegation is a secret that, when applied properly, can be a great parenting tool. The key to delegation is to perform it fairly and follow up. Every parent knows that each of their children has different abilities and capacities. It's important to remember that, when delegating responsibility, those who can handle more responsibilities around the house should be given more and those who can't handle as much responsibility should be given less. Fair delegation doesn't mean that each child will have the same amount of chores or responsibilities—it means that each child will participate at a level appropriate to his or her age and abilities. Delegation also doesn't mean that we, as parents, should sit back while our children become our little house-cleaning fairies. We should be actively involved in the responsibilities at home and delegate ourselves a fair part of those responsibilities. It's easier to hold kids accountable when they see us as fellow workers and not bosses.

Delegation isn't the only way to help families work together. During Jerrick's second year of college, he roomed with five other men in a small apartment. Each man was busy with school, most had a part-time job on top of that, and all tried to have a social life (*tried* is the key word there). As you would expect in such a situation, the apartment didn't stay clean for long.

They tried chore charts to divide responsibilities, but those didn't work. It wasn't that the men didn't want a clean apartment. Everyone tried to accomplish his responsibilities, but it was sporadic at best. One thing most children undervalue is the benefit of everyone doing his or her chores at the same time in order to create a clean house. The apartment always had the feel of a dirty apartment because one thing or another wasn't clean.

One day, a roommate came home to find another roommate preparing for a date by cleaning the kitchen and jamming out to some music. The roommates teamed together to clean the kitchen. This snowballed into a new way to clean the apartment. Every Friday, one roommate would start cleaning and turn on the music. When the other roommates heard the music they would stop what they were doing and join in. This way, the entire apartment got cleaned, just in time for the girls to come visit during the weekend!

Every one of Jerrick's roommates had something else he could have been doing. They were all exhausted from school and work during the week, and they all had homework and studying to do. Regardless, they all helped each other. The key was doing it together. An effective way for parents to make sure all chores are done in the house is to simply create a to-do list of what needs to be cleaned around the house and have all the family work together until the list is completed, like how Jerrick and his roommates worked together to clean their apartment. You'll find that the unity you feel as a family will deepen as you all work toward finishing chores together at the same time.

Sometimes, a father might come home from a particularly exhausting day at work to find his wife exhausted from watching after sick children. When both husband and wife expect the other to get dinner going, tempers might flare. That's when it is important to remember there is just work that needs to be done, and we do it together. Go turn on some music and get to it.

[MOTIVATING FACTORS]

Most people are not like the cheerful princess Snow White, whistling to music while we work. There will be conflicts and complainers. It's normal for family members—parents and children—to sometimes not want to help with household chores. After all, an object at rest tends to stay at rest, and resting is so much easier than working. These are some simple strategies parents can use to get every member of the family up and helping with household chores.

Jerrick was a very competitive child (some might say he is still very competitive). To make chores fun for him, his mom would time him to see how fast he could get his chores done. After he was done, his mom would check and make sure everything was done correctly. Find a motivating factor for every member of the family, whether that's a sticker on the chore chart for little children once a chore is completed, a thank-you note for teens, a weekly treat for all children if all the chores are completed, or something else of your own invention.

Even more important than creating motivation, however, is outlining the reasons why we clean. If a child correctly understands that putting toys away will make it easier to find them the next time she wants to play, she might be more willing to clean up after herself. Then we are starting to get beyond stickers and candy as the only motivations.

Household chores are excellent ways for parents to teach their children to take on new responsibilities. Once one child masters how to dust, show that child how to vacuum. Keep rotating chores so everyone gets a chance to learn how to do everything that is required to keep a clean house. Not only does everyone learn new skills, but no one gets bored by only doing one thing. When it comes to chores, having a variety is helpful to keep spirits high.

"Are we there yet?" No, we actually have quite a way to go on our family trip, and the car is going to get messy from all the food stops, French fries, and snacks. It'll be necessary to stop and clean the car every once in a while, and when that happens, the secret is to work together by sharing the load and splitting the work fairly between parents and children. When we learn that secret, our family journey will be more enjoyable because the car will be clean, but more importantly, because we'll all be learning to work together.

[PRINCIPLES OF ACTION]

How can you make sure everyone helps around the house? Here are some important considerations:

> » **The Bathroom Dilemma:** How can you apply the motto, "There's just work that needs to be done, and we do it together," in your own family?

> » **Working Together:** A chore chart is one way to make sure everyone works together to finish household chores. What other ways have you found helpful to encourage everyone to work together and follow up on delegated responsibilities?

> » **Motivating Factors:** Think about what motivates you to do something you don't want to do. What are some ways you can motivate family members to keep up with household chores?

[SECRET #10]

PINPOINT SOURCES OF SELF-ESTEEM

Low self-esteem paralyzes some people and keeps them from doing positive things with their lives. The victim might be our child or our spouse; it might even be us. We need to know the main sources of self-esteem and build our own feelings of self-worth as we help our family members feel better about themselves, too.

"Sing us a song," the young people were calling to a girl in their group at a youth conference where teenagers were putting on a spur-of-the-moment talent show as they waited for the dance to begin. Some young women had sung songs and a few young men had told jokes and done impersonations. Now they were coaxing one of the young women to sing. "Come on, you have a great voice," they said. "Sing the song we learned yesterday."

The young woman's embarrassment was evident. Everyone began to feel uncomfortable. Quickly, some of the young men stood up and sang a couple silly children's songs, complete with actions. The entire group was laughing and involved. No one noticed a youth leader seek out the embarrassed girl. This leader asked, "Is everything alright?"

"I hate it when my friends do that," the girl replied.

"They were just trying to make you feel good."

"I'm a horrible singer," the girl said angrily. "If I got up there, I would totally bomb."

The leader didn't say any more. She simply listened as the girl's feelings came gushing out. "I can't do anything right. I'm ugly and fat, and I'm the dumbest person in my school."

Just then, the group called to the girl and the leader to come be in some pictures. The girl stood up and started to leave the room. The leader said, "Don't go. Come stand by me. I would love to have a picture with you."

"No one wants a picture of me," was the response. "I wish cameras had never been invented. I hate cameras." The girl hurried out of the room, and as the leader watched her leave, she sensed that the real problem had very little to do with hating cameras.

Self-esteem is the mental picture we have of ourselves, the value we place on ourselves. Basically, it is how friendly we feel toward ourselves. Many people struggle to maintain a high and positive self-esteem. When we have healthy attitudes about ourselves, it is much easier to overcome problems. That healthy attitude helps us look at life with a positive outlook; we become sure of ourselves and our abilities. We do better in work, in school, at home, and in all aspects of our lives.

Low self-esteem seems to stop people from doing the positive things that will give them the very confidence they lack. They are often vulnerable, unsure, and negative. They attempt to mask their insecurities by withdrawing or becoming braggarts or even violent bullies. Still, their insecurities are usually obvious. Low self-esteem is related to poor mental health, poor academic or work achievement, as well as delinquency and criminal behavior.

Self-esteem is like the oxygen tubes that engage during plane emergencies. Have you ever wondered why flight attendants advise passengers to secure their own oxygen masks first before they help their children? When passengers take a few extra seconds to secure their own oxygen masks first, they are in a better position to help others. Self-esteem often functions the same way. When we, as parents, focus first on securing our own self-esteem, we are then better able to help our children with theirs.

Based on our experiences, and partially adapted from Nathaniel Branden's *The Six Pillars of Self-Esteem*, we have focused on the following eight secrets of self-esteem:[i]

[SOCIAL ACCEPTANCE]

Social acceptance is a sense of belonging that is influenced by what others think and say about us. In addition to friends, we are also influenced by the messages communicated to us by our own parents, coworkers, relatives, and leaders. That seems pretty straightforward until you realize that what people are actually saying or thinking does not really affect self-esteem so much as what we perceive is being said and thought.

One woman was born and raised in Texas. She remembers hearing her aunt, for whom she was named, saying such things about her as "Look at that girl's ears. They stick out like Dumbo's. I guess she's just naturally funny looking."

The same woman also remembers wearing a turquoise and white striped blouse and black skirt on the first day of fifth grade. As she was going out the front door, her mother remarked, "You have a figure just like a sausage."

The summer before this woman entered seventh grade, she grew to the height she is today—five foot ten. "I changed schools that year," she remembers, "and there I was on the first day of school, walking through the halls just trying to get my arms and legs going in the same direction. I was trying to work the combination on my lock when the head cheerleader came around the corner, looked down at my feet, and exclaimed, 'Golly!' Then she ran around the corner and called to her friend, 'Kathy, get over here quick. Check out these feet!'"

This woman had one best friend all through school. She had the same height and build and also had big feet. They were nicknamed "the Bobsey twins." They hated being taller than all the boys. Their mothers kept telling them, "Don't worry, the boys will grow," but it seemed to the woman that when she and her friend finally got to high school, the boys hadn't grown a bit.

Years later, the mother listened to her daughter's memories and was surprised when she told some of these stories. "Did I really say that you have a figure like a sausage?" she asked.

"Yes, you did," the woman replied.

"Well, you know I really didn't mean it like that. I just meant that you didn't quite have a waistline." But that is not how the woman heard her mother's comments.

"And I don't remember your aunt saying that your ears stuck out like Dumbo's," her mother continued. But the woman thought her ears stuck out like an elephant's, so she heard whatever her aunt had said as validation of what she already believed about herself.

Finally, the mother said, "You were not five foot ten in the seventh grade. You didn't get that last spurt of height until you were entering high school."

The woman said, "Mother, I felt as if I were six foot ten. All the boys and most of the girls were so much shorter. I tried slouching on one hip so I wouldn't feel so tall. I tried ducking my head down when I walked. My height was a problem I faced the whole time I was growing up." But the problem did not necessarily stem from her height so much as it stemmed from how she viewed herself.

This woman eventually learned to look past those perceived slights, and they do not currently affect her self-esteem. Many of us have learned to do the same, but some parents might harbor low self-esteem due to the fact that they still hold onto perceived notions of what others thought of them in the past. We may even have social acceptance issues now—in the workplace, in our volunteer activities, or even in our personal relationships—that might interfere with high self-esteem and will interfere with our ability to help our children with their self-esteem issues.

We suggest focusing on the positives to overcome those negative feelings associated with social acceptance issues. Try writing a few things that you like about yourself in your journal every day. Then, look for things you like about others and compliment them. You'd be surprised at how different your perception of each day will be when you focus on the positives within yourself and within others.

[PERFORMANCE]

Self-esteem is also based on performance. Again, it is not actually how we perform our work, but how we perceive we are doing.

A girl once appeared in a beauty pageant in California. She was not selected as the winner. She was not one of the top finalists. However, she felt she had done her best. In a letter to the mother of another contestant, she wrote, "Thank you for sending me those pictures. I had a wonderful time at the pageant, and I hope your daughter did, too. I learned so much, and even though I wasn't in the top ten, I know that I did my very best. I feel like a winner inside because I had the courage to try and I did all that I could." As this letter illustrates, self-esteem is usually not dependent upon winning so much as upon participating and doing one's best. The contestant who won could easily feel bad if she did not feel good about her performance—crown or no crown.

Brad attended a lecture at which the presenter said that, to build self-esteem in students, teachers must find something in which each one could excel. "There has to be something that each person can do better than anyone else," he explained.

Brad disagreed. He felt that such an expectation was both unrealistic and unnecessary. We do not need to continually measure ourselves against others in order to feel good. Self-esteem does not depend on trophies, high grades, money, job promotions, or winning. We can measure where we are now against where we once were and feel successful. An old Hindu proverb says: "There is nothing noble in being superior to some other person—true nobility is in being superior to your own previous self." It might be nice to be number one in something, but that is not a requirement for self-esteem. We just need to feel we are doing something right and well.

[OPEN COMMUNICATION]

A man had a drinking problem at one point during his life. However, he gave it up later. This man and his wife knew that their son had high self-esteem when he wrote: "Thank you, Dad, for giving up alcohol after drinking for forty years. That is an unforgettable example to me that we can all make positive changes. I feel that my worst habit is laziness, and I'm trying to conquer it. I will conquer it, just watch and see."

Like this young man, as we practice open communication with our spouse and children, we will develop high self-esteem. Open communication, however, doesn't mean using degrading or offensive remarks to get our point across. Those remarks only reveal our low self-esteem because we feel we have to attack others, lowering theirs.

Jerrick remembers working in the food service industry as a delivery boy during his first few years in college. He hadn't been working there very long when he accidentally put double the needed amount of hot chocolate mix in a five gallon thermos. The customers came back livid because their hot chocolate was, to put it nicely, thick.

After Jerrick's supervisor pacified the patrons, he pulled Jerrick aside to talk. First, the supervisor told Jerrick what a great job he'd been doing so far by specifically naming things he'd done right. Then, he asked Jerrick what happened. After the explanation, this supervisor reprimanded Jerrick for not following directions, but ended the talk by telling Jerrick how happy he was to have Jerrick as an employee. Rather than feeling low, Jerrick felt like his self-esteem had been raised because he knew that his boss believed in him.

As we learn to give positive comments and to correct in an uplifting way when correction is needed, we will develop high self-esteem—in ourselves and in others.

[SHOWING EMOTIONS]

Picture a room crowded with teenagers. First, the young women are asked, "OK, ladies, pretend you're on a date with a guy and something really sensitive happens and tears start coming down his cheeks. What would you do?" By this time, every young man in the room is tensing up and feeling embarrassed. But nearly all the young women sigh, and then one of them blurts out, "We like it when guys show their feelings." The guys are surprised. They have never dreamed that young women would understand. They thought it wasn't OK to show emotion, especially around young women.

Jerrick's grandpa on his mother's side passed away when Jerrick was eight years old. He doesn't remember much about the funeral, but he does remember sitting in the pew next to his mother. Jerrick's uncle was singing a beautiful song, and Jerrick started to tear up. *No, I'm not going to cry,* he thought. *Babies cry, and I'm not a baby.* As if he had spoken those thoughts out loud, Jerrick's mom turned to him, and with tears on her face, said, "It's OK to cry."

The water works were opened, and Jerrick remembers crying during the rest of the funeral. He also remembers his mom's arm around his shoulder, pulling his head close to her, and crying along with him.

If we can cry during appropriate times in front of family members, then our self-esteem is pretty high. If we hold everything in, we have some improving to do in this area, but we can improve. Just remember, "It's OK to cry."

[DISTINGUISHING BETWEEN THE REAL AND THE IDEAL]

In today's world, we are constantly barraged with ideals that are unreal. We can't turn around without another image of fitness, beauty, talent, and perfection being thrust upon us. It's easy to feel defeated if we try to look as great as the people on television and in movies.

We may wonder why we can't sing and dance the way people do on TV without getting worn out and winded. We don't realize that the programs we watch are filmed over several days and that the performers are usually lip-synching because their dance routines are so challenging.

Magazine covers continually place pictures of the ideal before us. One magazine cover featuring the face of a popular movie star stated in the caption that this particular woman needed "absolutely nothing" to be beautiful. The following month, however, another magazine offered proof that even this beautiful star needed a little help. The retoucher's bill for the picture on the cover of the first magazine had been obtained, and it seems the beauty who needed "absolutely nothing" ran up a bill of $1,525 for retouching her photo.[ii]

Though it is difficult, we must keep in perspective the pressures imposed by others. We are asking for problems if we begin to internalize such expectations. When the ideal becomes self-imposed, we tend to hear comments like these: "I just have to get skinny, or no one will like me," or "I have to get this promotion, or my family won't respect me."

Try asking family members to rate themselves on a scale of one to ten, with ten being the ideal. Most people will put themselves at a five. That's normal and not terrible at all until the most significant people in their lives start insinuating, "That's not good enough. You have to be a ten, and it has to happen right now." One young man's grandmother told him, "You have to do better in school because I want you to be a success. I want you to be a doctor like your father and uncles. Your brothers didn't make it, and none of your cousins made it. You're my last hope."

Those types of comments can diminish the successes of the family members toward whom the comments were directed. Rather than feeling proud of what they have accomplished, they begin to feel weighed down by what they haven't, and self-esteem starts to plummet. But imagine what could happen if instead a completely different statement was made: "A five is good; there's nothing terrible about that right now. You have the potential to be a ten down the road. We believe in you." A little positive encouragement can go a long way toward increasing a family member's self-esteem.

[PHYSICAL WELL-BEING]

Sometimes, after several days of vacation, a mom might say to her children, "I'm going to bed. You can stay up for a little bit, but make sure you still get a good night's sleep. We have a busy day tomorrow." It wouldn't be a stretch to imagine this scene that next morning: Children groaning and whining because they stayed up most of the night playing games and eating junk food. They would feel terrible. We all know that same feeling too well.

Compare that feeling to what is expressed in a letter from a young man named Michael: "Last year, I was seriously thinking about suicide. . . . I was unpopular in school, ate lunch alone, and was a little 'chunky.' I also felt very depressed and unloved. This year, I decided to get rid of the sad, depressed me. I lost fifteen pounds and got a job. . . . Now I feel as if a fifty-pound jacket has been lifted off my back."

We are proud of this young man. He has made some positive changes in his life. He feels better and is more hopeful and in control of himself. As he has worked at being more healthy, he has come to feel better about himself in other areas of his life as well.

When we, as parents, work toward being healthier, we will also feel better about ourselves. We don't need to get back into high school shape; that's unrealistic. We can focus on getting enough exercise each week to help ourselves feel healthier. Exercise can reduce stress levels, diminish fatigue, and even improve our quality of sleep. We will feel better about ourselves as we exercise, and our self-esteem will improve. We can encourage our children to do the same.

[AVOIDING COMPARISONS]

Several years ago, a counselor met a young man named Paul. Paul's parents were concerned about his self-esteem, so they called this counselor and asked if they could fly their son out to California to work with her for a week. She agreed, and so Paul went to stay in her home. At first, their conversations went something like this:

"What do you like to do? Do you like sports?"

"No. I hate sports."

"How about school? Do you like school?"

"No, not really."

After several other similar exchanges, she finally asked him, "What do you do when you get home from school?"

"Play the piano."

"What kind of things do you play?"

They went into the living room of the counselor's home, and Paul sat at the piano and played a beautiful piece of music that he had composed.

"Incredible!" the image consultant exclaimed. "Look at the talent you have!"

"Yeah, but not like my brother," Paul replied. "He plays football." He then showed her a picture of his brother—the muscular captain of the high school football team. Paul was spending a lot of time comparing himself with his brother. He acted as if his piano playing was not important.

A first reaction in trying to help Paul feel better might have been to start pointing out the imperfections in his brother, but this consultant knew that trying to make others look bad never makes us feel good for long. Paul had to shine brightly by recognizing and cultivating his own gifts, not by dimming the lights around him.

Paul worked on overcoming his negative attitude about himself. After a few years, he sent the image consultant the cover of his first recording—an entire album of original compositions, with a great-looking photo of Paul on the front. It was entitled "Paul Anderson: Himself."

[APPEARANCE]

As many times as we are told that the inside is what really counts, there is no escaping the fact that we base much of our self-esteem on appearance. Most people are acutely aware of how they look. They agonize about their complexions and being over- or underweight. They can usually pinpoint a few things they like about how they look and then provide long, detailed lists of defects, real or imagined. One girl wrote: "My last two boyfriends broke up with me because they didn't want their friends thinking that they were going out with such an ugly girl."

Not only is our self-esteem affected by our own appearance, it is also affected by the appearance of family members, friends, and their belongings. A dad laughs about the time when he drove his children to high school, and they asked to be dropped off three blocks away from the building because they didn't want their friends to see their dad's old, beat-up Volkswagen bus.

People in every stage of life may measure their self-esteem by what they see in the mirror. There is nothing wrong with that as long as we don't compare what we see in the mirror to other people. As we focus on our own appearance and not on the appearance of others, we can make positive changes, and our self-esteem will be higher because of it.

[WHICH MATTERS MOST?]

Of these eight sources of self-esteem, which matters the most? Is it appearance or physical well-being? Is it performance or social acceptance? What is the main source of self-esteem? It is difficult to pinpoint just one source because people usually draw from a combination of these sources, along with others unique to them individually. However, these sources offer a basic framework on which we can build understanding.

"I wish cameras had never been invented. I hate pictures," the insecure young woman at the dance said. However, the pictures that cause her frustration are not the ones taken with cameras. Rather, they are the ones she has developed in her own mind. Unfortunately, when she felt that way, her self-esteem pictures were out-of-focus, fuzzy, and cloudy.

Each of us must see clear pictures of ourselves—our true beauty, greatness, and potential.

Again, we may find ourselves asking the question, "Are we there yet?" We're afraid not. It's easy to become discouraged and get down on ourselves when the journey doesn't go according to plan. Flat tires, empty gas tanks, or mechanical issues can deflate our enthusiasm for the trip in the same way that poor self-esteem can deflate our personal happiness. Instead, we need to replace the tire, fill up the gas tank, or fix the mechanical issues in our trip, and we need to recognize the sources of self-esteem in our lives so we can strengthen it in ourselves and build it in those we love. The secret is that feeling good about ourselves will help us reach our destination and enjoy the trip.

[PRINCIPLES OF ACTION]

How can you have higher self-esteem and help others have higher self-esteem? Here are some elements to keep in mind:

» **Social Acceptance:** Examine other family members and ask yourself, "Do they feel like they belong?" Think of how you can help them feel more accepted and valued.

» **Performance:** Self-esteem isn't based on how others feel you're doing but on how you feel you're doing. How is your self-esteem affected when you feel you've performed well?

» **Open Communication:** Good communication skills are a sign of high self-esteem. How could you communicate better with others?

» **Showing Emotions:** Think of someone you know who has difficulty showing emotions. How could you help him or her recognize that showing emotion is a healthy practice?

» **Distinguishing between the Real and the Ideal:** Often, people need positive encouragement to distinguish between their own potential and the ideals that society establishes. What can you do to show positive encouragement when a family member struggles?

» **Physical Well-Being:** High self-esteem is often associated with being healthy. What goals can you make to help you become healthier?

» **Avoiding Comparisons:** Each individual has his or her own abilities. What can you do to develop your own talents? How can you help your children develop theirs?

» **Appearance:** When was the last time you complimented someone's appearance? How specific was that compliment? How would that help someone with low self-esteem?

» **Which Matters Most:** Considering these sources of self-esteem, which would you like to work on, and why?

[ENDNOTES]

i. Nathaniel Branden, *The Six Pillars of Self-Esteem* (New York: Bantam Books, 1994).

ii. Goldring, Stacey. "Makeup: We All Need It." *The News.* Boca Raton. 4 Dec. 1990. Print.

[SECRET #11]

BUILD SELF-ESTEEM BY BEING P-A-R-E-N-T-S

Parents have a direct and powerful influence on how their children see themselves. Once we have control over our own self-esteem, how can we help those who suffer from low self-esteem? What are some specific things we can do to help them feel better about themselves? Here are some secrets that you can remember by thinking about the letters of the word P-A-R-E-N-T-S.

["P" STANDS FOR "PRAISE"]

A young man wrote, "My parents support me one hundred percent. They are always there for me. As we grew up, my brothers and I participated in sports. My mother was at every one of our games. Mom and Dad are always there cheering us on when we get down."

Another young man wrote, "I wish my parents would praise me more. I hear, 'You can do better' a lot more than I hear 'That's really good.' I hear a lot more negatives than positives, and I think it should be the other way around."

In their book *Counseling, a Guide to Helping Others,* authors Terrance D. Olson and R. Lanier Britsch write, "One reason children feel inadequate is that their adequacy has never been acknowledged by the adults in their lives."[i]

Praise feeds the soul just as food feeds the body. You know how much food children's growing bodies can take in. How much food are we offering their growing souls? A kind word can help children keep their guard up against drug usage, alcoholism, and unwanted pregnancies.

One particular girl, by her own admission, was not a very good student in high school. Nevertheless, she had enthusiasm that wouldn't quit. Her parents kept their attention and comments directed to their daughter's strong points, telling her, "You are the sunshine of our home."

Another mother found that, when she complimented her daughter, it helped not only to be specific but also to look for distinctive and creative ways to express her feelings. For instance, once she left a note and candy bar on her daughter's bed. Another time she took out a personal ad in the local paper that read: "To Jessica—You brighten my day. Love, Mom."

One girl attended cosmetology school. She did exceptionally well, even taking first place in a state hair-design competition. That day, she called her mom excitedly and said, "Mom, guess what?" After sharing her good news, she added, "I knew you'd be happy to hear this." She wasn't calling to brag about her accomplishments. She called because she knew that her mother would want to hear about her success and that she would praise her. She was right.

One form of praise found to be particularly effective is to create positive nicknames for family members. A boy named Dan might become "Dan the Man." Ben might be called "Big Ben." Ray becomes "The King" and Linda is "Pretty" because that is what those names mean in Spanish.

In some cases, positive nicknames can be a sign of acceptance and help children feel approved of and important. One boy said, "One thing my dad does that really helps me is when I play football, he calls me 'Mr. Touchdown.'" When Jerrick played volleyball in high school, his nicknames ranged from "Slinky" to "The Wall of Jericho" to simply "Huge." Having those nicknames helped him have confidence in his athletic abilities, even when he couldn't see those abilities himself because of his own struggling self-esteem.

Some people believe that liberal amounts of praise make children feel arrogant and conceited. On the contrary, it builds confidence and security. There are enough influences outside the home that point out faults. Young people don't need parents and family members to "keep them humble." Often, most people do that to themselves. Children with low self-esteem tend to bring themselves down when no one is looking. Instead of seeing themselves in the mirror and saying positive things like "Today is going to be a great day," they might say things like, "Look at your hair! Who could ever fall in love with you?" or "No wonder no one likes you. Look at all that acne." The confidence and security that children with low self-esteem need aren't going to come from themselves; it's going to come from the praise of parents and family members.

One dad, after complimenting his daughter, received what he thought to be a verbal slap in the face. He had said, "You look nice tonight." The girl responded, "No I don't. You're only saying that because you're supposed to."

Young people who do not feel good about themselves usually do not know how to receive compliments well. When compliments are rejected, we need to see through built-up defenses and remember that when people are starving, sometimes they reject the food they so badly need. If public compliments don't work, try complimenting in private in the future. Some children don't like public praise because of the potential negative social stigma attached to being recognized before a group. One young man put it this way, "I'm proud of getting straight A's in school, but I don't want anyone to announce my grades over the loudspeaker because then the other kids start calling me 'The Brain.'"

A teacher named Randy Bird told about a young man in his class who, when Mr. Bird asked for reports from the students on how much they had read, would reply that he hadn't read beyond the first chapter. At the end of the term, he told Mr. Bird in private, "I just thought you'd like to know that I've finished the whole book."

"Why didn't you tell me sooner?" Mr. Bird asked.

The young man, who was a state-champion wrestler and very popular with his peers, responded, "I didn't want people to know I like to read."

Negative comments seem to come so easily: "You move like a turtle." "How many times must I tell you that you just don't look good in that outfit?" Ralph Waldo Emerson said, "Words are as hard as cannon balls."[ii] Our children feel those cannon balls when we casually or thoughtlessly say, "You're so stupid," "You really give me gray hairs," or "I just can never count on you. I knew I'd end up doing your work." We must be careful. It is human nature for people to live up to what is said to and about them.

Mother Teresa has said, "Kind words can be short and easy to speak, but their echoes are truly endless." Brad's wife, Debi, has never forgotten an occasion in her teenage years when someone told her that, in a meeting, a leader had praised her for her dependability. While the leader didn't pay the compliment directly to Debi, she learned about it, and the words made a real difference in her self-esteem.

A young man named Matthew from Illinois once said, "I love it when parents and leaders praise me for the things I have accomplished, big or small. Some people think you outgrow the need for that, but I don't think anyone ever outgrows the need to be praised."

["A" STANDS FOR "ACCEPT"]

A young woman wrote, "I wish my parents could more readily accept who I am instead of who they want me to be. They should encourage me in the activities I enjoy instead of always demanding that I do the things they want."

Growing up is a time for experiencing new things. This is obvious in everything from the music and dress to the types of extracurricular activities family members select. As long as standards are not compromised, parents should give children space and accept the choices they make. We need to let others express their opinions and feelings freely.

One mother said, "My husband and I were not very happy when our son decided to get so heavily involved in sports in high school. We knew that, in the long run, he would be better off putting his efforts toward getting better grades and preparing for college. But we listened to his point of view and accepted his decision."

Young people must never feel that parents accept them only when they do things their way. They must feel they are accepted for who they are and that they are always regarded as individuals of great worth and potential, regardless of whether or not we think their present choices and actions are worthwhile.

When a certain couple got married, the husband said to his new wife, "There's 80 percent of me that's good and 20 percent that's not so good. If you choose to dwell on my 80 percent, we're going to be happy." The same is true of children. We need to dwell on their good qualities and help them to feel that we truly accept them for who they are.

A young man said, "My parents are always picking at me about something. It's like they want me to be perfect—and they want it right now." A sixteen-year-old Korean American youth said that everyone has the idea that "all Asians are smart. Having a reputation for brains is nice, I guess, but it can also be a pain. My father and mother expect an awful lot out of me. They want me to be number one." Another young woman wrote, "I am the oldest of many children. My father is a leader in the community, and I'm expected to be the perfect example for my brothers and sisters and friends. Sometimes my parents expect me to excel in everything I do and never be mediocre."

Sometimes we hear the counsel, "Don't be mediocre." However, we should also remember that the word *mediocre* comes from the Latin word *medioasis*, which means "halfway up the mountain." Mediocrity is not bad so long as it is not the final goal. Mediocrity is simply a halfway point through which everyone must pass on the way up the mountain. We all have to be mediocre before we can be anything beyond that.

Maybe our kid isn't winning any contests. Maybe he or she isn't getting top grades. Maybe he or she is "mediocre." Well, what's so wrong with that? We're talking about children and teens. Right now is the time when they are supposed to be going through mediocrity in many areas as they learn and grow. Perhaps a young man wants to be in debate, but his father wants him to be a track star. Maybe another young man is interested in car engines while his mother would rather have him developing his skills with people. Our children need to have opportunities to develop their own interests and talents. And having a messy room today doesn't mean a child's future home will always be messy. Wearing wrinkled clothes today doesn't mean a teenager will dress inappropriately for his or her first job interview.

One young man put it this way: "I wish my parents understood that my effort doesn't always correlate with my achievement. Sometimes I put forth a lot of effort and don't always have great achievement. But that achievement, however small, is a success for me because I am trying and not giving up. I don't mind high expectations being put on me because that keeps me striving. But when expectations are too high or unrealistic, it is discouraging."

["R" STANDS FOR "RESPECT"]

"I wish my parents understood that the things I do are just because I'm an individual," a teenager said. "I wish they understood that I am me, and my little brother is separate from me. We're two different people."

Brad knows a woman who has coached five young women who have won the title of Miss USA. It surprised him to find out that her coaching does not involve teaching young women how to fit into the mold of a beauty queen. Rather, she helps them to discover and accentuate the things that are unique to them. That's what makes them winners.

One of these young ladies is Michelle Royer, who represented Texas at the national competition. As she was getting ready to go to the Miss USA pageant, where she ultimately won the crown, she wrote to her coach:

"I never could really put into words how much I appreciate you or how much I've grown in the past few months. When people ask me how you've helped me, I tell them that, besides giving me Texas on a silver platter, you've given me the opportunity to learn on my own. Never before have I been able to rely so much on myself. That's a pretty good feeling, considering the next month ahead of me. It sure feels good not to be scared any more. Some of my so-called friends in school and in other beauty pageants made me, or should I say I let them make me, feel insecure because I never fit into their mold. You taught me there is no mold for Michelle Royer. I'm the only one, thank goodness. I hope that you'll be proud of me when I compete in the Miss USA pageant."

Michelle's coach believes that one of the reasons Michelle won the pageant that year was because she figured out that she is a unique person while the others were still trying to be whatever they thought the judges wanted. The people who met Michelle and talked with her admired her confidence and relaxed manner. People respected her for her individuality.

Brad grew up in a family of all boys and no girls. He recalls that, "My brothers all happened to be good athletes. I was not. My dad respected that. He expected me to learn how to handle a ball. He taught me how to catch, throw, dribble, and pass. But beyond that, he respected what I wanted to do. I attended my brothers' games and athletic events. They, in turn, attended my school plays and music recitals. I got negative put-downs at school for not being a very good ballplayer, and I always felt uncomfortable when we would play basketball in P.E. classes. The thing that got me through all of that was being able to come home to a safe place where parents and family respected me for my strengths and talents."

One young woman said, "My mother once compared my sister to me. She said something like, 'Well, you aren't getting the grades that your sister got.' My sister really hated it when my mother said that. Such comparisons accomplish nothing. They do not motivate the child being talked to, and they do not reinforce or uplift the child being talked about. It's a losing situation in every respect."

["E" STANDS FOR "ENCOURAGE"]

A teenager offered some good advice for all parents: "Parents could compliment us on the little things and boost our egos up and encourage us. They could say, 'You can do whatever it is you want to do. We believe in you. It doesn't matter if you win. Just have fun!'"

When Sharlene Wells Hawkes competed for Miss America, she had some pretty discouraging times. Since the competitors usually stand in alphabetical order, as Miss Utah, Sharlene was always standing next to Miss Texas, who wore designer outfits and expensive jewelry. (As Miss Utah, Sharlene had won a simple, inexpensive wardrobe from a chain department store.) Many times, photographers would say, "Please move over, Miss Utah, so we can take a few pictures of Miss Texas." Sharlene would back out of the way. It was embarrassing.

On the night of the parade on the famous boardwalk at Atlantic City, New Jersey, where the pageant was held, each contestant had an opportunity to sit in a convertible and wave to the crowd while photographers took her picture and reporters interviewed her. When Miss Texas sat in the car, many flashes from the cameras went off and interviewers asked lots of questions. When it was Sharlene's turn, she sat in the convertible in her department store dress and raised her hand to wave—but there was not one flash, not one question.

Sharlene walked back to the hotel and felt like crying. Then she bit her lip and told herself, "Oh, no you don't, Sharlene. You have two things that you can count on. One is your belief in yourself. The second is the fact that your family is behind you."

Her parents had taught her to believe in herself and to count on her family. Their support and encouragement were consistent and unwavering. Had Sharlene not won the title of Miss America, she still would have come away from that pageant secure in the support of her family. She was a winner either way, and because she won the pageant, she became a winner both ways.

Sometimes even our smallest attempts to encourage family members can go a long way. A young man named Chris said, "I really love my parents. They support and encourage me in everything I do, and that is what probably helps me the most. When I feel that encouragement, it makes me feel that I don't have to go out and drink or party. It gives me self-confidence so I can overcome peer pressure. I don't think I'd be the kind of person I am without the encouragement and support of my parents."

["N" STANDS FOR "NOTICE"]

"Instead of always asking me to do more around the house, I wish my parents would thank me for what I've done and maybe notice that I'm trying to help," a teenager wrote.

One father said, "When my children got older, I realized quickly that I needed to have eyes in the back of my head. Now I guess I need to train those eyes to see the positive and ignore the negative. It's too easy sometimes to look at the dirt on the flower's petal rather than the beauty of the flower."

A woman once told of a little experiment she tried with her son. Rather than continuing to nag him as she had done for months for being moody around the house, she decided to simply compliment him when he did better. When he took out the garbage, she said, "Thank you." When his report card came home with mostly A's and B's but one D, she forced herself to say, "That's great that you have so many high grades" instead of jumping on him about the low grade that first caught her eye. At the end of several weeks, she reported, "He is doing much better and his countenance has brightened around the house. All this time I kept thinking that my job was to change him and his attitude, but it was I who needed to change first." She smiled when she added, "I am finally learning to catch him doing something right instead of doing something wrong."

Along with noticing the good things family members do, it is also important to notice when they need to talk or open up. One girl told Brad, "My dad may not always be the most sensitive person in the world, but when something is really bothering me, he always seems to notice. He'll come up to my room and say, 'Want to talk about it?' I always say, 'How did you know something was wrong?' and he just smiles."

["T" STANDS FOR "TIME"]

Some studies have indicated that, on average, parents spend less than ten minutes a day talking with each of their children. And much of that talking is harsh, judgmental, and critical. Remember the old radio spot: "So you want to build relationships with your kids? Take your time."

Many families find that the only way to bring busy lives together is to make time rather than wait for time. One father said, "I look at it this way. If I were invited to attend a dinner at the White House or to do something else I really wanted to do, that strong desire would alter my schedule. I would simply make time for it. It is said that good intentions will never replace good attentions."

Setting one night a week apart for time together as a family will give you the opportunity to really get to know your children. They may say they don't like it, but they do. Brad has a daughter named Wendee. When she was in second grade and he asked what her favorite part of school was, she said, "Recess."

Brad asked, "What do you do at recess?"

"Chase the boys."

"What do you do when you catch the boys?"

"We take them to jail."

"What do you do with them when they are in jail?"

"We hug 'em."

Brad said, "Wendee, you'd better stop that. The boys don't like it."

She said, "Daddy, they say they don't like it, but they do."

Even though children may resist at first, they really do like it when parents and leaders spend time with them. Time together can reduce the influences of the outside world and increase the influences we have on each other.

Try surprising family members with a picnic at a park or "kidnapping" them and taking them to a show. Once, a mother picked up her daughter and her daughter's best friend for a surprise lunch during the school day. When her two children were growing up, that same mother would occasionally give them a special day when they got to go anywhere they wanted to go with her. Her daughter once wanted to go to the beauty parlor and get a manicure. They did it. Her son wanted to go to a popular shopping center to have ice cream and chocolate chip cookies for breakfast. They did it.

Brad tells of an experience he had raising his family. "My wife and I spent several years overseas with our family while the kids were growing up. We both look back at those times as wonderful bonding experiences. My wife says that the reason it was great was not just because we were involved with other cultures, but because we were together with our family more. We became very close as a family and learned to depend on them. That time together made a difference."

["S" STANDS FOR "SAY"]

"The thing I have the hardest time with is that my parents still treat me like I'm a baby," one young man lamented. "It's as if I can't be trusted to do anything on my own, and what I think or want to do makes no difference, even if I have a good idea."

When Jerrick was in eighth grade, one of his household chores was mowing the lawn. He remembers talking with a friend at school about how much he despised having to wake up early on Saturday just to mow the lawn before it got too hot outside.

"I wish I could mow my lawn," this friend sadly commented. "My parents won't let me. They think I'll cut my toe off."

"Have you asked them to teach you?" Jerrick asked.

"They won't do it; they never let me do anything," his friend answered.

Parents need to give children a say in the things that affect them and their lives. They must be able to express their opinions, give input, make changes, and affect their environment. We must offer them a voice in deciding on the nature and complexity of their goals.

One father of eight children said, "Kids need guidelines, and when I have to say no, I'm not afraid to say it. In my job, I have guidelines, and people say no to me a lot. But within those guidelines, I also have freedom in my work, a sense of ownership that makes what I do fulfilling and satisfying. That's the same kind of balance and ownership I try to offer my children."

P-A-R-E-N-T-S. As easily as we can spell the word, we can remember to build self-esteem in children by praising, accepting, respecting, encouraging, noticing, spending time with them, and giving them a say in their lives. Each of these suggestions may have to be tailored to fit individual circumstances, for just as each child is unique, so each will react differently. But as we seek to do our best, the secret is that we can find unique ways to tailor our actions and responses so that the self-esteem of those children and teenagers for whom we are responsible will improve.

"Are we there yet?" Believe it or not, we're getting closer to our destination of a happier family, but it's still a ways away. There are long stretches of road that can test our patience, and we may find our children getting uneasy. Likewise, we may also find our children with low self-esteem because of long stretches of rough patches in their life. If we remember the secrets that P-A-R-E-N-T-S stands for, we can help our children during those hard times. Our children will then have improved self-esteem, and the trip to family happiness will be much easier and more enjoyable for them and for us.

[PRINCIPLES OF ACTION]

How can you have an influence on the way your children view themselves? Here are some suggestions:

» **Praise:** Think of what your children did today. How could you praise them for their efforts in a way that would be memorable?

» **Accept:** What are some ways that you could show your children you accept their individual interests and activities?

» **Respect:** How do you show your children that you respect them?

» **Encourage:** Think of a time in your life when helpful encouragement boosted your self-esteem. Who provided it, and why did those encouraging words have that effect on you?

» **Notice:** During the next week, pay special attention to one or two little things that your children do for you. How can you show them you notice and appreciate their kindness?

» **Time:** Look at your daily activities and determine how much time you really spend with your children. What are some ways that you could increase the time spent together?

» **Say:** What are some ways you could let your children have a say in the choices that affect them?

[ENDNOTES]

i. R. Lanier Britsch and Terrance D. Olson, *Counseling, A Guide to Helping Others* (Salt Lake City: Deseret Book: 1983).

ii. Ralph Waldo Emerson, "Self Reliance," *Essays: First Series* (Stilwell, KS: Digireads.com 2007), 17-30.

[SECRET #12]

KEEP LOOKING FORWARD

In ancient Greek and Roman mythology, the phoenix is a beautiful flying creature with a gold and scarlet tail. It lives for five hundred years as a spectacle of inspiration for all who view it. After its years are completed, the phoenix builds a nest. According to a Roman poet named Ovid, the phoenix then collects "cinnamon, and spikenard, and myrrh" which then ignite in self-consuming fire. The phoenix is turned to ashes, but from those ashes a new phoenix is born.[i]

We know a man who works as a firefighter. One day, this firefighter was dispatched to the scene of a dirt bike accident. Imagine his shock when he arrived at the scene and discovered that the victim was his own teenage son. During the wreck, the handlebars of the dirt bike had crushed the boy's chest, severely injuring his heart, lungs, and ribcage. The boy was rushed to a local hospital where doctors performed emergency life-saving surgery on him. Unfortunately, he is now partially paralyzed from the waist down and can't walk without assistance.

This teenager was athletic, very involved in his local high school, and popular with his peers. The accident was his own personal phoenix fire. He said, "The doctors said I would never walk again and the remainder of my life would be spent in a wheelchair. My life as I knew it was over, but this is when my new life started." The teenager's old life ended with the accident, but like the phoenix, he emerged from the accident as a new person. This boy is now grown up, married with a family, and working on a doctorate. His family members—both his new family and his parents and siblings—continue to learn and grow closer together as a result of the accident.

Life can throw us curveballs. We could be driving along on our dirt bike, and suddenly our lives could be changed forever. In those situations, the secret is to learn from the phoenix and create a new life. The phoenix gathered cinnamon, spikenard, and myrrh to facilitate the growth of its new life. When we or members of our family are faced with severe challenges, we can look to the future, endure with patience, and serve with love to facilitate the growth of our new life.

[LOOK TO THE FUTURE]

In the popular novel, *The Lord of the Rings*, the protagonist of the story—Frodo Baggins—wishes that the nearly impossible task entrusted to him "need not have happened." His mentor and friend, Gandalf, responds, "And so do all who live to see such times. But that is not for them to decide. All we have to decide is what to do with the time that is given to us."[ii]

There will be times in our lives when we will wish that a certain situation "need not have happened." During those times, it is important to remember that what's done is done and life is what it is. We can't change the situation that happened, and now we have to decide what to do with it. During Frodo's darkest hour, when he was about to quit, his friend Sam says, "Even darkness must pass. A new day will come. And when the sun shines it will shine out the clearer. . . . There's some good in this world."[iii]

Our trials can be seen as temporary setbacks. When the new day comes, the trials will pass, and our lives will be clearer because of them. Occasionally, a setback might be permanent, like that of our friend becoming paralyzed. But even with such a major life challenge, there was still something good for our friend to look forward to. The same will be true for all of us. There will still be some good in this world—even in a new and different life. We should seek out the good and look forward to it.

Jerrick's dad had a friend in high school named Laney. Laney was popular, a tri-sport athlete who took state in wrestling three years in a row. He later attended college and nursing school, got married, and started a family. When Laney was in the prime of his life, he was diagnosed with Lou Gehrig's disease, a disease that affects nerve cells in the brain, eventually leading to paralysis, loss of motor skills, and death.

Laney valiantly fought the disease for over twelve years, but eventually succumbed to its effects. He was unable to move or speak for ten of those years, but "he completed many personal histories, prepared a lifetime of memories for his daughter, pursued his family genealogy, and always updated family and friends with a monthly newsletter. He did this through the help of his many helpers and visitors."

Jerrick was still a child when he met Laney for the first and only time. Laney was very frail, confined to a wheelchair, and couldn't speak. Jerrick's dad put his hand on Laney's shoulder and said hello. His dad and Laney looked at each other for a few seconds and smiled. Laney's smile was full of hope and gratitude. Jerrick's dad stayed in touch with Laney and introduced him to his children. Even though Laney could only give head nods in response, that contagious smile never left his face. Jerrick can still see it in his mind. Laney was faced with insurmountable obstacles, but he was still able to find many things in his life to look forward to and "Laney accomplished more in his twelve years of sickness than most people do in a lifetime."[iv]

No matter the trial, no matter the setback, parents can learn to look to the future and help their family members do the same when trials occur. There's no doubt it will be difficult, but look to the example of Laney. Even the largest and darkest of clouds will be blown away by winds of change, and the sun "will shine out the clearer."

[ENDURE WITH PATIENCE]

A Roman Emperor named Marcus Aurelius wrote, "All men are made one for another . . . bear with them."[v] It doesn't matter whether we're the one faced with a personal setback or if we're the family member of a person who is struggling through a trial or if it is simply a person we know from work or the community, all of the people involved need to bear it together and endure with patience.

A certain family we know is a great example of enduring with patience. One of the boys in the family was goofing around in his room with some friends who were not paying attention when the boy became entangled in a cord and began to suffocate. Although the boy survived, he has to live with permanent changes to his life. The boy can no longer speak, walk, or take care of himself. That burden has been placed on his family, but rather than shrinking from the task, the family has tackled it head on.

Every day, family members help the boy get dressed, go to the bathroom, and feed himself. They do everything in their power to make him as comfortable as possible. The task sometimes becomes too great for the family alone, so they have enlisted help from friends and extended family. Jerrick considers himself privileged to have been given the opportunity to help this family and their son. Every time he is able to go help move the boy into his bed or onto his scooter, he leaves with a greater appreciation for the positive attitude this entire family exhibits toward their shared trial. He has never heard them complain. They endure with patience and have made the best of a difficult situation, which, in turn, is making them all better people.

[SERVE WITH LOVE]

In each of these stories, the situations these good people have been faced with are made easier through service. One father was able to serve his son by providing medical care to him immediately after his dirt bike accident. Their entire family served during the recovery process. Laney had visitors who would come talk to him, keep him company, and help him work on his newsletters and family history, and the entire community became involved with taking care of a boy who almost suffocated.

Mahatma Gandhi lived by this truth: "The best way to find yourself is to lose yourself in the service of others."[vi] It is important for us to serve those who are faced with severe ailments in their lives, but it is also just as important for those of us who are directly affected by a trial to lose ourselves in the service of others. Often, providing service to others—in whatever ways we are able—can help us find our new selves when faced with the prospect of starting a new life and trying to adapt to difficult circumstances.

We know a woman who suffered a stroke a few years ago. The stroke left her with limited motor skills and unable to do most of the things she used to enjoy. Even so, she still finds the time to volunteer at a local food bank. It helps her focus on others and not just her own limitations.

Jerrick's great-grandmother started going blind many years ago. She used to enjoy painting beautiful pictures, but now she could barely see their outlines. Instead of painting, she found other ways to serve others.

She enjoyed researching her family history, and Jerrick would often visit his great-grandmother only to find her slouched over pieces of paper with a giant magnifying glass. She was reading old birth records or journal entries. She would carefully record the information she found so that others could benefit from it. That service activity helped her focus on other things rather than her diminishing eyesight. We can all find ways to help others, even if it's following the example of Laney and just smiling at them. Serving others—especially our family—with love may not diminish our own problems, but it will make them easier to handle.

One of our friends has a son who was diagnosed with cancer during his early teenage years. He has been fighting this disease for many months, but the numerous surgeries and rounds of chemotherapy have taken their toll, not on the cancer itself, but on the morale of the boy and his family. His parents and siblings have valiantly served him during his ordeal, and they have found that their service not only helps raise the boy's spirits but also raises their own spirits. His parents especially treasure the time spent serving their son because of the memories they are creating with him, and now some of the son's sweetest memories are of his family showing their love to him through service. The family and the boy are raising each other's spirits—together.

As parents, we can all have similar experiences with our children. Even in their darkest hours, the secret is to keep looking forward. We can yet create some of our sweetest memories.

"Are we there yet?" Not quite. The stormy weather of life has caused a road closure, and we must chart a new path. In such cases, we can be like a phoenix, which rises from its own ashes and starts a new life. When faced with life-changing obstacles, we can still move forward. We can rise from the ashes and create a new life for ourselves and those we love by looking to the future, enduring with patience, and serving with love.

[PRINCIPLES OF ACTION]

How can you rise from the ashes of difficult family struggles? Here are a few keys to think about:

» **Look to the Future:** What are some things you'd like to accomplish in the next five years? The next ten?

» **Endure with Patience:** Think of a time when you weren't sure if you'd be able to get through something difficult. What helped you get through it?

» **Serve with Love:** How does serving others help you keep your own problems in perspective?

[ENDNOTES]

i. R. van den Broek, *The Myth of the Phoenix according to Classical and Early Christian Traditions*, Trans. I. Seeger (E. J. Brill, 1972).

ii. J. R. R. Tolkien, *The Fellowship of the Ring, being the First Part of the Lord of the Rings* (New York: Ballantine Books, 2012).

iii. J. R. R. Tolkien, *The Return of the King, being the Third Part of the Lord of the Rings* (New York: Ballantine Books, 2012).

iv. "DeLane 'Laney' Johnson Jr.", Obituary (3 Jun 2008), http://boards.ancestry.com/topics.Obits2/1398/mb.ashx.

v. Marcus Aurelius, *Meditations*, Trans. Gregory Hays (New York: Random House, 2002).

vi. Mahatma Gandhi, *Wisdom for the Soul: Five Millennia of Prescriptions for Spiritual Healing*, Ed. Larry Chang (Washington: Gnosophia, 2006), 626.

[SECRET #13]

FACE THE STORMS
OF LIFE TOGETHER

During a visit to Arizona, a motivational speaker was invited to stay in the home of a man and his family. The speaker met two small children in the family and also a teenager who was introduced as the man's sister. Later, the man explained, "My sister is here with us because she got into so much trouble at her old school that my parents felt that it might be best for her to move to a new school and get a fresh start."

"How is it going?" the speaker asked.

"Oh, she has managed to get into plenty of trouble here, too," said the man. "She has a drug addiction. At first we wouldn't let her go anywhere without one of us with her. But my wife and I couldn't keep that up. It was killing all of us."

"So, how did you handle it?"

"I sat my sister down and explained that we were wrong to be watching her constantly. It was as if we had been keeping her in a box and feeding her through a little hole in the top. I told her that from then on, we were going to love her, prepare her, teach her, and then let her decide what she will do and face the consequences."

The speaker was interested in the man's reasoning and asked, "How did your sister respond to that?"

"It's been stormy, but she is making it. Her progress is slow, but she is further along than she was."

Like this man, anyone who deals with children realizes quickly that not only can't we stop the storms they face, we can't completely shelter them from those storms either. The secret is to offer a support system—an umbrella against the rain. To do this, we must learn how to open the umbrella. We must know what is happening in the lives of our children, recognize signs of stress in them, and know how to deal with our own stress as parents.

[KNOW WHAT IS HAPPENING]

"I wish my parents would talk to me about sex and stuff," a teenager said. "Whenever I bring up the subject, they just get scared. It's like they want to lock me up in the house and not let me go out. They don't realize that it's out there, and there's no escaping it. I just wish they would confront the issues I'm dealing with in my life instead of avoiding them and pretending that the problems will go away."

To be informed, it is important that we know what is happening in the lives of our children. "My children didn't always make it easy for me to stay involved in their lives," one particular mom states. "They have become social critics. Suddenly I can do nothing right. I don't wear cool clothes, and I don't have a cool car. They don't want me to meet their friends. It seems I'm an embarrassment to them." As children grow and desire to fit in, such an attitude is to be expected. Still, rejection is tough to take. This mom continues: "I wanted to pull away from my children, since that is what they seemed to want. But I thought about it and determined that sometimes what teens want and what they need are different things. I am their mother, and whether they admit it or not, they still need me."

She clarified, "Don't get me wrong. I don't follow them around with a video camera. But I know who their friends are. I know their class schedules. I know their teachers. I find out what is going on at school. I follow them on Facebook." Like this mom, we must be informed. Learn the facts about drugs, alcohol, smoking, and the music that kids like to listen to. When they watch TV or go to movies, try to keep up on what they are seeing. Follow them on social networking sites and monitor screen time. Adults will never be allowed to join the teenage world totally. That wouldn't even be desirable. But we can be informed enough that we know what is happening in their world. Knowing what's out there prepares us to offer shelter when we sense a gathering storm.

[RECOGNIZE SIGNS OF STRESS]

Some signs of stress are easy to see. Some are more difficult. Easy signs include fatigue, tenseness, restlessness, crying, inconsistent sleep and appetite patterns, frequent colds or headaches, persistent worrying, lashing out in anger, ignoring physical appearance, erratic achievement—good one week, poor the next. (That sounds like college!) Most of us can relate. We know these signs from experience.

Signs of stress that are more difficult to spot and interpret are avoidance strategies, such as daydreaming or standing around on the sidelines and not getting involved in activities. Another sign of stress is passive resistance, when a child takes on an "I-don't-care-so-nothing-can-really-hurt-me" attitude. Another sign to watch for is when teens are constantly on the go. And when they don't get enough rest and struggle with how to say no to negative peer pressure, it's a sure signal that they are not handling their stress appropriately.

Brad knows a young man who is intelligent and athletic. In his senior year of high school, he began faltering. His parents worried. Their son was within a few requirements of completing his Eagle rank in scouting, but suddenly he didn't want to finish it. He had the grades and test scores to receive scholarships from almost any university in the country, but he wouldn't fill out the applications. His sudden lack of motivation bothered them a great deal. They pushed him harder, and he withdrew further.

An advisor recognized the boy's behavior as a sign of stress. One day, the leader pulled the boy aside to talk to him. At first, the boy was true to the "I-don't-care" attitude he had put on. However, the more they talked, the more his anxiety surfaced. He said that he would be graduating soon, and he didn't know what career he wanted to pursue. His parents expected him to attend college, but he thought general education classes were a waste of time. He didn't want to finish his Eagle requirements because he knew he had made some mistakes and really wasn't worthy to be held up as an example to younger boys.

After the talk, the leader spoke to the boy's father and pointed out the stress the boy was experiencing right now. The father decided to back off for a while.

Slowly, things improved. He finally completed some college applications, even though he was too late to qualify for the scholarships he might have received. Everything seemed to be going better except, interestingly enough, the boy's relationship with the advisor faltered. Now the boy wouldn't talk to him. He avoided eye contact with him and would rudely walk away whenever the leader attempted to say hello.

The leader felt bad. What had he said to offend the young man? Such behavior continued for weeks. Finally, he realized that this, too, was a sign of stress. The boy had opened up to him, and consequently, he knew things about the youth that no one else knew. Perhaps he shouldn't have shared them without permission—even with the young man's father.

Mistakes that have not been properly resolved can cause a great deal of pressure and stress. Regrets of the past that have not been properly faced can rob the present and future of peace, joy, and vitality. The leader concluded that one day, when the boy corrected his mistakes, he may also be able to face him again, too.

[LEARN TO MANAGE STRESS]

One young woman wrote, "Sometimes my parents have a bad day, and then they get upset and mad. I can understand this because I have bad days, too—everyone does. It's just that when they are angry and snapping at me all the time, I begin to take it personally and start thinking that I've done something wrong."

Another young woman wrote, "My parents need to realize that if they bottle up their financial problems inside of them, they may think they are saving the family from having to face them, but it's really harder that way. Their problems still affect the attitude of the family, but if mom and dad will not talk about them, then we don't know what is really wrong, and we start thinking they hate us."

Part of helping family members deal with stress is to be aware of our own stress. Few jobs are as stressful as parenting. Trying to balance the demands of children, work, personal needs, and other responsibilities can seem endless and overwhelming. One mother said, "By the time I combine the lack of support I receive from my ex-husband with my financial worries and the myth of the 'perfect' family, I don't feel that I have anything left to offer my kids."

Another mother said, "I have to take some time for me. It is a pain and sometimes causes more stress than it relieves, but I have found that if I just take a brief time to exercise or read, I can turn my attention back to my children with better results." When parents let stress get the best of them, their children don't get their best.

Two young women wrote to a friend about their home life. Consider how much easier it would be for these teenagers if their parents learned how to handle their own stress more appropriately.

The first writer said, "My mother has multiple sclerosis and has been in a nursing home since I can remember. My dad, because of this, has demanded perfection from me in everything I do. His comments about me never living up to his expectations have pushed me into drinking, drugs, and six attempts at suicide since I was twelve."

The second young woman wrote, "I feel rejected at home. I'm seriously considering running away. My mother is never home because both my parents work. That wouldn't be so bad except my dad is always yelling at me and my two brothers to clean up our rooms or wash the dishes or vacuum while he just stares at those dumb football players in the dumb football game on TV. Our house never has the Christmas spirit, even on Christmas. This year, my parents were so stressed out on Christmas Eve that everyone ended up in a bad mood."

Help is available for parents from many sources. Information on the topic of stress management is plentiful. However, as with many things, most of us already know what we should do. It's just a matter of doing it. The secret lies in a Japanese proverb that says, "If we simply deal with the problem, the problem becomes simple."

"Are we there yet?" Not yet, but we'll get there. We ran into a storm, and our windows won't roll up. We're starting to get soaked, and the roads are slippery, but don't worry. We're pulling out an umbrella, and the skies look clear ahead!

[PRINCIPLES OF ACTION]

How can you help shelter family members from the storms of life? Be careful not to overlook these suggestions:

» **Know What Is Happening:** Think of a time in your own life when you have been able to avoid problems by knowing what was going on. What were you aware of at that time?

» **Recognize Signs of Stress**: What are some of the signs of stress you have recognized in the past when dealing with those you love?

» **Learn to Manage Your Own Stress:** What is one activity you usually engage in when you feel stressed? What are other activities that could help?

[SECRET #14]

SHOW YOUR LOVE

"I would like to talk with my dad about girls and stuff because he is a guy, and I think he would understand," one young man said, "but I don't ever feel like he has time for me. When I say, 'Dad, can we talk?' he just rolls his eyes, looks at his watch, and says, 'Well, OK. So what's so important that we have to talk about it right now?' It totally kills my enthusiasm."

It's no secret that young children need someone to care for them, but as they grow they also need someone to care about them. Children can face anything if they know we are interested in them and care about them. As parents, we can fulfill that need. The secret is to show your love. We must express love verbally, but we can also show we care as we listen to our children and allow them to talk out their frustrations. We can also make a conscious effort to evaluate our own expectations, and we can help children confront their fears.

[LISTEN WITH EMPATHY]

Ruth stormed into the house and slammed the door furiously. The wall shook, and the light fixture swung back and forth. Her father wasn't usually home this early. To her surprise, Ruth heard him start down the hall from his study. She could tell he was upset at how hard she had slammed the door. But before he could give her his usual lecture about "don't break it unless you can afford to fix it," he heard her crying. He asked, "Hey, what's with the tears?"

Ruth said, "I don't want to talk about it." She started walking past him toward her room.

He stopped her. "Come on, tell me what's wrong."

Ruth felt more comfortable talking with her mother, but right then she was so frustrated that she was willing to tell anyone. She turned to her father and sobbed, "It's just awful. There is this kid at school and he is really popular. He has been eating lunch with me and my friends. Well, he's not very good at math and stuff." Ruth was struggling to get the words out. "So I've been helping him with a big assignment that was due in Mr. Ivan's class, and the guy kept saying that he didn't understand how to do it. Yesterday he asked if he could have my answers. I didn't know what to say, so . . . "

Her father picked it up from there: "You gave him your answers."

Ruth nodded and went on. "But that's not all. Mr. Ivan found out, and the principal put us both on academic probation. He said he's not going to let me graduate. The story has gone around the whole school now. It's awful."

Her father's first inclination was to criticize his daughter's actions, but he restrained himself and remained quiet. In his mind, a small debate was happening. He was feeling two roles: father and friend.

The father inside him wanted to get upset and say, "Well, this is your own fault, young lady. You should never have given him your answers in the first place. I hope you learn a lesson from this." The friend inside him said, "How would I handle this situation if this were not my daughter but another young woman coming to me for advice?" The father in him was upset at Ruth for letting this happen, perturbed that she didn't have more backbone when it came to peer pressure, and concerned for Ruth's reputation and future. The friend was feeling Ruth's pain, empathizing with her vulnerability, wanting very much to comfort her and dry her tears.

Ruth's father moved closer to his daughter and hugged her tightly. "Don't worry, honey. We'll get this straightened out. Let's call the principal tonight."

Ruth knew there would be consequences to face for her choice, but things finally did get straightened out just as her father said they would. Perhaps the best thing that came out of the whole experience had nothing to do with school. She later said, "I didn't want to tell my dad what happened because he has never been very good at listening. He's too quick with advice. But that day I found out that when I really needed him, my dad was there for me, and he really did understand."

It's always easier to be patient and understanding when it's someone else's child. Even with our own children, it is usually much easier for them to be friends with other adults and accept their advice. Sometimes young people feel safer talking with someone who is not close enough to react with shock or anger to the things they say.

In the same way, it's also easier to listen to the problems of someone who is not so close to you. For example, if the girl next door came over and confided that she was pregnant, most of us would try to be understanding and calmly help her see what her next steps need to be. We certainly wouldn't be yelling in anger or feeling hurt and betrayed. But if that girl were our own daughter, it would be more difficult to control emotions and personal reactions. The closer we are to the person, the more responsible we feel. That's why a good rule of thumb to remember is that when children talk over their problems with us as their parents, we need to treat them as well as we would treat our neighbor's child. Think friend first and then parent. That's one way to show our love.

[HAVE REALISTIC EXPECTATIONS]

A schoolteacher in Georgia has the following rules posted on her classroom wall:

1. We are all learning here.
2. Making mistakes is OK.
3. You don't have to know everything today.
4. Intelligent people ask for help.

Think how comfortable you would feel as a parent if your child were enrolled in such an environment. What guidelines are posted on our walls? What expectations are we communicating?

A young woman wrote the following letter: "I'm fifteen, and I feel like I'm trapped in a jail with my own family. I live with my dad, my older half-brother, and my younger brother. My sister lives with my mom in another place. My problem is that I don't know how to tell my dad that I have feelings too and that he is expecting too much of me. If I ask him if I can spend some time with my friends, he tells me to clean the house. I could ask my brothers to help, but they are like my dad and think that cooking and cleaning are women's work. My dad just sits in front of the computer while I work. I feel like I'm my dad's wife when I'm only his daughter. How do I tell him that I'm only fifteen? I can't do all this stuff by myself and keep up in school, too."

Another young woman wrote, "I wish my parents would stop nagging me about little things. They should be grateful I'm such a good kid instead of always expecting more. I know I'm not perfect and that I have a lot of room for growth, but it seems like I can never please them."

While some children may benefit from having their levels of anxiety increased by adults, the majority of them do better if adults will help them lower their anxiety levels. Words such as "It's OK, everyone makes mistakes," "Nobody is perfect," and "Just take it one step at a time" may seem trite to us, but they go a long way in helping children. Having and communicating realistic expectations is one way to show our love.

[CONFRONT FEARS]

A mother told about a time when her son was asked to speak in a school assembly. "He was terrified," she said. "He doesn't think of himself as much of a public speaker, and he hates big crowds. He is much happier being with animals than people."

As the big day drew closer, the mother recognized all the signs of stress. In fact, they weren't just signs; they were massive electronic billboards. She tried to help. She was willing to listen, but he was in no mood to talk to her. She assured him that it didn't matter what he said in the talk; she was already proud of him for being willing to do it. Nothing she did or said seemed to help.

Finally, on the day before the assembly, she tapped on his bedroom door. He said, "Come in." She entered to find him surrounded by books and wadded-up papers. His tenseness and nervousness were obvious. She asked, "Look, what's the worst thing that could happen?"

"I'll make an idiot of myself."

"What can we do to handle that?" Her tone showed confidence in his ability to cope. She was treating his fear with respect.

"Well, would you listen to what I've written so far?"

She was surprised at the request. If she had suggested the same thing, he probably would have told her to get lost. She listened intently, praised him generously, and offered a few suggestions.

The following day, the young man gave an excellent speech. His mother said, "It was short but wonderful. He spoke effectively. The principal even commented on how well he did, which made him feel on top of the world. I was really relieved and happy that it turned out as a good experience."

Once "the worst thing that could happen" is out in the open, it can be demystified. Panic and fear become less intense. When family members are able to admit the truth and say the unsayable, the problem isn't solved, but the sting has been taken away. Helping children confront fears is one way to show our love.

"Are we there yet?" No, we aren't. In fact, our children are having emotional meltdowns in the backseat. The trip has been long, the A/C isn't working right, and they are getting restless for attention. The storms we've encountered have even made them scared. To make the trip enjoyable, we can listen to them, adjust our own expectations for the trip, and help our children confront their fears. The secret is to show our love. Just hang in there a little bit longer, and we'll reach the destination.

[PRINCIPLES OF ACTION]

Along with saying "I love you," how can you show your family members that you care? Here are some suggestions:

> » **Listen with Empathy:** Think of a time when a family member listened to you. How did that make you feel? How did you know that he or she was truly listening?
>
> » **Have Realistic Expectations:** What do you expect from your family members? How do those expectations show you care?
>
> » **Confront Fears:** Think of a pressing fear that a family member may have. How can you help him or her overcome that fear?

[SECRET #15]

BE IN TUNE WITH YOUR FAMILY

"My parents and leaders talk about peer pressure as if it is something that all these gang members put on all the good kids," a young man said. "That is not the case with me at all. Every negative experience I have had with peer pressure has been from good kids, from my friends."

The secret is to be in tune with your family. When we, as parents, discover that secret, we can help children deal with the pressures they encounter. We must take individual circumstances into account, but however minor or severe the problems, we should always encourage young people to draw perspective from others and to lean on someone stronger.

[DRAW PERSPECTIVE FROM GOOD EXAMPLES]

Good examples can give us a deep well from which to draw perspective when the pressure hits. Often, those examples will come not from the media, but from the lives of people we know. One of Jerrick's greatest examples comes from a family that he knows and loves. Jerry and Colleen are construction workers who were faced with difficult circumstances some years ago. Around 2007, America was hit with a horrible economic downturn, and Jerry and Colleen were severely affected by it. Their construction business suffered, and any savings that the couple had managed to build quickly disappeared. Month after month, they struggled to pay the bills, but they never struggled with keeping a positive outlook on life.

In the midst of a very trying and stressful time for the couple, they decided to quit smoking. Not only did that decision save the couple a lot of money, it also provided extra motivation to keep going. They figured that if they could quit smoking, they could do anything. As their financial struggles persisted, they continued to maintain that same positive outlook. They countered every difficult situation with positive changes in their lives. To this day, they will tell anyone who will listen that the hardships they faced during those trying years led them on a happier path in life because of their willingness to maintain a positive attitude.

A few years ago when Jerrick was faced with unemployment, he looked toward Jerry and Colleen as an example of how to handle that situation. Their positive attitude helped Jerrick gain strength as he searched for jobs.

When Jerrick and his wife have children, they plan to use this experience to teach them the importance of good examples. As parents, we can look for times in our lives when we drew strength from good examples to get through a particularly difficult problem or trial. We can use those times to teach our children the importance of finding and following the good examples in their lives.

[LEAN ON SOMEONE STRONGER]

Children need to realize that however difficult the pressures they face may be, they can find someone who can be a support. As parents, we need to be among the people our children can lean on when the need arises.

About two weeks after getting his driver's license, Jerrick decided to take a different way to school—just because he could. He turned onto a street near his school and was driving what he thought was the speed limit, about 35 mph. He noticed a policeman behind him and thought to himself, *I'm going the speed limit and wearing my seatbelt; this cop's got nothing on me.* It turned out the cop knew something Jerrick didn't—the actual speed limit. Forget the speakers in Jerrick's car, once he saw those lights turn on behind him, Jerrick's heart was beating as loudly as the subwoofer.

After giving the cop his information, Jerrick received a ticket in exchange. On the front of the ticket was a court date that was mandatory to attend, and Jerrick figured he would be going to jail! Or at least, that's what he thought. In reality, Jerrick just had to appear in court, but how was he to know that? He hadn't experienced getting a ticket before. He turned right around and drove back home. In that moment, all he wanted was his parents to tell him it was OK. Because Jerrick always had an open relationship with his parents, he knew they wouldn't yell at him. They might be disappointed, but they would help him learn from his mistake—or at least visit him in jail.

Jerrick's parents listened calmly as he explained the situation. When he got to the part about how he was going to jail because the ticket said he was to appear in court, they laughed. Between chuckles, they assured their son that everything would be OK. Jerrick's mom told him what a "court appearance" actually meant and assured him that his dad would go with him. His parents set up a payment plan so Jerrick could pay back the ticket and even suggested that his younger sister go to traffic school with him because it would be a good experience for both of them. Jerrick's parents knew from experience what to do, and Jerrick was able to lean on them.

Sometimes we, as parents, may not be strong enough by ourselves to offer support for our children. It may be difficult for us to give our children the shoulder they need to lean on because our shoulders are already carrying heavy loads. We can surely lean on other family members or a friend when the road seems long and we feel weak. Many of these friends have experienced similar struggles, and can help us in our journey.

We know a mother who has a child with a debilitating disease that makes it difficult for her child to walk. As she watches her child struggle, and as she tries to juggle her additional responsibilities in her home and at work, she sometimes finds the load too difficult to bear alone. However, this mother found a support group of individuals with children who have the same disease as her child, and that support group has lifted some of the burden off her shoulders. This group made it easier for her to provide the shoulder that her child desperately needed. Like this mother, we can find help and support through family, friends, and others who can strengthen our shoulders, making us better able to support our children through their struggles.

An eighteen-year-old young man named Jacob summed up the idea of being in tune nicely when he wrote this message to parents: "First of all, you have to open your eyes and realize how bad it is everywhere—at work, at school, in public. People are swearing, telling dirty jokes, and doing bad things. Don't try to shelter us from that, hoping you can keep the world from influencing us. That's impossible these days. Instead, educate us and prepare us before it's too late. Don't let our reluctance and complaining keep you from encouraging us to do the right things. Give us people to look up to and be there to help."

"Are we there yet?" Not yet. We're traveling down a long, boring stretch of road and can't tune in to any radio stations to keep us going. Even though the radio stations won't come through clearly, we can still find joy in the journey by tuning into each other. We can draw perspective from good examples and lean on others for support when we most need it.

[PRINCIPLES OF ACTION]

How can you be in tune with your children's lives and help them face thier problems? Here are two suggestions that could make a difference:

» **Draw Perspective from Good Examples:** Do your children have good examples they look up to? What more can you do to be a better example?

» **Lean on Someone Stronger:** Think of a time when you relied on someone stronger to get you through a trying moment. Why did you rely on that person? What specific things did he or she do to help?

[SECRET #16]

BROADEN YOUR VIEW

When Brad was a small boy, his family visited the pyramids in Egypt. He remembers, "As we approached the famous monuments, my parents were amazed at the sight. My older brothers were fascinated. But I couldn't see what all the fuss was about. I thought the hotel where we were staying was a lot nicer than these big, old, dusty things."

How the members of his family perceived the Egyptian pyramids made a big difference in how they valued them and acted toward them. The same is true with family members. Do we see our family members as the wonders of the world or simply wonder what in the world we are going to do with them?

Beliefs drive behavior. In working with children, we, as parents, must try to stretch our vision and see their grandeur. We must remember the potential of these young people, regardless of their current choices. And we must see our own efforts as parents as being worthwhile, even when we see no immediate outward evidence of their effectiveness. In viewing family members, the secret is to shift from telephoto lenses—which restrict our vision—to wide-angle lenses in order to broaden our view and see what we may otherwise have missed.

[SEE GREATNESS]

Family members can try us to the limits and exasperate us. One mother said, "My son makes me so mad that I'd like to use him for a piñata at the next party!" But then there are other moments—those shining Camelot moments when everything goes right and our hope is restored.

Jerrick participated in the scouting program when he was a teenager, and one of his Camelot moments came during a scout camping trip. He loved going on the hikes and campouts that the scout troop would put together. One particular hike involved using large hiking backpacks to carry supplies into the campsite.

"There were lots of us on this camping trip, and there was a pretty big age gap between the scouts," Jerrick remembers. "There were thirteen-year-olds clear up to seventeen-year-olds on this trip. The seventeen-year-old scouts had no problem with those backpacks, but some of the younger scouts were really struggling." Those scouts hadn't quite grown yet, and for one particular scout, the backpack was about as tall as he was. It certainly weighed as much as he did.

Jerrick was in a group lagging behind the first group that this young boy was in. The boy tried his best to keep up with the rest, but because of the weight of the backpack, the scout began to slow down. As Jerrick's group caught up, he could see the entire group circling around this young scout. The older scouts divided the weight from the young scout's backpack and helped carry those supplies up the mountain, in addition to their own backpacks. They weren't asked to do it, but they decided to help shoulder the load anyway.

In such a moment, we see greatness. As parents, we can see that greatness when our children pitch in and help with their siblings' chores. We can even see greatness when, like a young father of two boys that we know, we see our toddler offer to share his chocolate chip cookie with his brother. Chieko Okazaki has written, "When we learn that it is only with the heart that one can see rightly, we develop eyes to look upon the inward person. When we do this, we will discover a wonderful secret: Every person is, as it were, an angel in disguise."[i]

[SEE POTENTIAL]

Jay was a handsome young man, strong, athletic, and popular. Some people said that he was a young man who had everything going for him. But Jay's father, who knew his son better than others did, recognized many weaknesses along with the strengths. He said, "I finally had to take away his phone because he simply would not stop calling all the girls he would meet around the state at athletic events. He was costing me a fortune."

The father was also concerned at Jay's lack of attention to school-work and his attitude that he could get by well enough without giving his best effort. Their relationship suffered. Jay's father was putting up with Jay more than he was enjoying him. It was almost as if he had said to himself, "Just a few more years, and he'll be gone. I'll just endure till then."

Then a teacher came to Jay's dad. He spoke about how talented Jay was and how he felt like Jay has a great future ahead. Jay's dad was astonished when he heard this. It gave him a different view. During times of immaturity, Jay's father would think of the potential this teacher described and see his son through different eyes.

Working with children is a lot like opening presents; the fact that the packages are wrapped makes the experience all the better. It might be easier if everyone knew right up front what was in each box. There would be a lot less exchanging and guessing. By the same token, there would be a lot less joy. The possibilities, with all their surprises, make opening presents exciting and even enriching. When we are dealing with children, we must remember that many of their greatest gifts are still wrapped inside, waiting to be discovered.

During times when it seems hard to put up with our children, the secret is to see them as they are now, but also see what they can be in the future.

[SEE YOUR EFFORTS AS WORTHWHILE]

Brad attended a youth conference where one of the adult leaders brought a book to finish reading. During all the workshops, service projects, and dances, he sat off to the side and read. Later, he was encouraged to get involved with the youth, and he discovered the difference between giving his time and sharing himself.

At the end of the conference, the leader stood up and said in honesty, "I used to make up excuses to not be with young people because I felt awkward and unsure around them. But at this conference, I've learned that I do have something to offer. Now I'm going to start making excuses to be with the youth instead of the other way around."

Sincere efforts made for family members are never wasted. Whether our impact is recognized immediately or not, it is felt. Children live better lives when we share with them what is uniquely ours to offer. We must not underestimate the impact of a smile, a touch, a compliment, a funny joke, a shoulder to cry on, or a listening ear—all of which have the potential of being a turning point.

In junior high school, Jerrick had a science teacher named Mrs. White who was instrumental in shaping him. Even as a twelve-year-old boy, Jerrick could tell that Mrs. White truly cared about him and his classmates. She was different than many of the other teachers at the school. She started a science club, which Jerrick joined, and some of his fondest memories of junior high school were spent with that club taking care of their garden or preparing for Future City competitions in which students competed with other junior high schools to try to create the most environmentally friendly city.

Those competitions gave Jerrick a love of infrastructure and engineering. He kept in contact with Mrs. White throughout high school. She's now retired and living in a different state, but they still correspond via Facebook.

All through high school, and up until just a few years ago, Jerrick planned on going into engineering. Mrs. White was thrilled that he was continuing his education into a science field. However, Jerrick changed plans and decided to study English instead. He still loves engineering, infrastructure, and architecture, but isn't pursuing a career in any of those fields. Even though things didn't turn out the way Mrs. White might have wanted, she is still proud of the person Jerrick has become. In like manner, even though Jerrick is no longer actively involved in the sciences, he is still grateful for the influence that Mrs. White had and continues to have on his life. Her effort wasn't wasted.

One day, a nineteen-year-old man was cleaning out his bedroom in preparation for moving out of the house (much to the delight of his eager little brother), and the young man found some papers and reports he had saved from elementary school. He smiled as he remembered the fun he had had and the positive influence his teachers had been in his life. He thought, *I wonder if they even know how much they helped me.* That same day, he wrote to some of his favorite teachers to say thanks.

A few days later, a letter came from his second grade teacher. "You will never know how much your note meant to me," she wrote. "In all my years of teaching, I have rarely received such a wonderful uplift. I cried to think that anything I said and did those many years ago may have helped you. It is easy to become discouraged in this profession, wondering if you are making any difference at all. You made my day, my week, my year!"

At those times when life begins to seem like a never-ending string of advice no one listens to, meals no one appreciates, and good deeds no one acknowledges, we must switch to wide-angle lenses and broaden our view.

A crying baby in the middle of the night or a misbehaving child may need the most love at the very moment when they are least loveable. By broadening our view, we can continue to work with even the most difficult of children out of compassion.

At the end of our lives, we won't remember the cars we drove or the awards we received as much as we will remember the time we spent with family and friends. We will remember the efforts we made to help, lift, and love others.

Imagine a tourist looking at the Pyramids of Egypt, the Great Wall of China, or the Grand Canyon through only a telephoto lens. Think of all he or she would miss. To enjoy the broader beauty and significance of these wonders of the world, a wide-angle lens is required.

The same is true with our children. As we see their greatness and potential, and as we acknowledge the worth of our own efforts, then we have broadened our view with a wide-angle lens that allows us to see our children as the true wonders they are and will become.

"Are we there yet?" No, we're still traveling, and sometimes we get so focused on our destination that we don't take in the sights along the way. Although our destination will be wonderful and we are excited to arrive, there are important things to see along the way. As we stop and admire the scenery around us, our trip will become more enjoyable. Similarly, as we see greatness and potential in our children and acknowledge our own efforts, our trip to family happiness will be more joyful for everyone.

[PRINCIPLES OF ACTION]

How can you broaden your view of family members? Here are some reminders:

» **See Greatness:** Can you remember a time when a family member succeeded? What made that occasion so great?

» **See Potential:** Think of a time where you saw potential in a family member. What helped you see that potential? When have others seen potential in you?

» **See Your Efforts as Worthwhile:** How can you recognize that sincere efforts made for family members are worthwhile—even when things don't turn out quite as planned?

[ENDNOTES]

i. Chieko N. Okazaki, *Lighten Up!* (Salt Lake City: Deseret Book, 1993).

[SECRET #17]

KEEP ON TRYING

A man sat at his desk preparing a talk. He was going to speak at a funeral service. This task was nothing new. In fact, he had made similar preparations so many times before that he already had a filing cabinet full of appropriate comments and thoughts. But this time was different. He struggled, even agonized over what he should say. This time the talk was for the funeral of his own son, who had committed suicide a few days earlier.

Most people who knew him had noticed how rebellious the boy had become. Most of them had also seen the pain it was causing this good father. Still, no one was too worried about the situation. After all, he was a wonderful father, and the son had a good upbringing. Things would all work out right in the end—or so they thought. But the end had now come much sooner than anyone expected, and things hadn't worked out at all.

The man looked at the blank papers before him and began to cry. He felt sure there were no more tears to fall. Hadn't he used them all up in the last few days? Yet, once again, they came flooding down his cheeks. No one would ever know the sorrow that filled him. The guilt and failure he felt were profound.

Just then, there was a slight tap at the office door. The man sat up and wiped his eyes with the back of his hand. "Come in," he called. A woman entered the room. She was helping to make some of the funeral arrangements, but upon seeing the man, she knew it wasn't a good time. She turned to leave. He said, "Please don't go. I don't want to be alone right now."

She wondered what to say. It seemed all the regular words, such as "I'm so sorry," and "Time heals all wounds," had already been said too many times by too many people. Quietly, the woman said, "I don't know much about these sorts of things, but I do know that sometimes all you can do is still not enough."

The man said nothing. The woman left the room, but her words lingered: "Sometimes all you can do is still not enough." Strangely, those words brought the first comfort the man had felt for days. He and his wife were only human. All they could do as parents was to try their best, and if this was one of those times when their best was still not enough, then the matter was out of their hands. The man turned back to his papers and began to write his talk, starting with the secret this woman just told him, "Sometimes all you can do is still not enough . . . "

[HANG IN AND HANG ON]

A mother wrote to Brad from Japan, where her family lived because of a military assignment. Her letter was not legible in places because her tears had blurred the ink. She and her husband were doing all in their power to help their struggling daughter, but still she was making poor choices.

All Brad could write in response was, "Hang in and hang on." He told her that we must remember that sometimes even the greatest diligence on our part is insufficient—at least temporarily—against the effects of others' freedom. Children sometimes make unwise choices, and at those times, perhaps we can only have faith in their ability to change, keep loving them, and hang on. But we can't get down on ourselves.

One woman approached Brad after a class he taught. Her heart was broken. She said, "I don't even know why I came. I just feel so full of guilt."

"What's wrong?" Brad asked.

"A few months ago, my son made some wrong choices. He had consequences from those choices, and remains totally unchanged and bitter." She started to cry. "I've done all I can. So has his father," she explained through her sobs.

"Then you have no reason to feel guilty," Brad said. "Your boy does, but you don't."

"But I must have done something wrong somewhere along the line, or things would never have turned out like this."

Later, Brad received a letter from this same mother. She was still full of grief. "I have given and given of myself to that kid," she wrote. "I've gone so many extra miles for him, I could never count them all. It's not fair that boys from negative and abusive homes can become good men while my husband and I do everything we can to help our son and he blows it." She felt humiliated and embarrassed.

We must never forget that we cannot completely control another's freedom, nor should we try. It was the young man himself who had chosen to do wrong. Perhaps he rationalized about it, trying to justify his actions. Perhaps he was blaming others or even pretending that what he did really wasn't wrong or that he "didn't know any better." But ultimately, he is accountable for his own actions. Don't give up! Children can still find a way to see things clearly, choose the right, and overcome misbehavior if they so choose. We must continually try to teach and persuade them in love, but they also have a part to play.

[DO YOUR PART]

Any influence we can have upon others—including our own children—depends upon two parts. We must do our part, and the others must do theirs. It's much like a ladder resting on a wall. If one leg happens to give way when someone is on it, is it the fault of the other leg that stood strong?

Sometimes we as parents condemn ourselves if our children struggle. However, in a world of free people, where there is knowledge, accountability, opportunity, ability, and responsibility, choices ultimately rest squarely on the shoulders of those who make them.

The mother of the boy who made wrong choices later wrote another letter. She said: "Things are going better. My husband and I are slowly learning how to choose happiness independent of the actions or attitudes of anyone else—including our son. It will be hard to erase the hurt, and there are still feelings of guilt, but we decided we must face this challenge with perspective."

Curt Galke tells of an experience that happened to him when he was training to be a doctor. As part of his residency, he was working in a hospital emergency room when several teenagers who had been in a knife fight were brought in. Curt was assigned to work on a boy who appeared to be about fifteen. He had two or three stab wounds that would need to be closed, but the one that worried Curt the most was a small puncture wound on the left side of the boy's chest. Suddenly, the boy's pulse dropped, and there were dangerous changes in his blood pressure. Curt and the emergency room doctor he was working with concluded that a knife must have penetrated the boy's heart and left a hole that was bleeding.

Curt says, "The doctor moved quickly. Making sure the boy was adequately sedated, he took a scalpel and made an incision from the breastbone around to the boy's back. He spread the patient's ribs apart and asked me to reach into the chest and pull his heart to the surface so we could examine it. I did as I was asked. I couldn't believe it. I actually had a young man's heart beating in my hand."

Curt and the doctor found the hole and repaired it. You would think that the youth would never have survived such an ordeal, but he did. Curt stayed with him until he awoke in intensive care. Curt imagined his first words would be, "Gee, thanks," or "My chest hurts!" Instead, the boy's first words were "Did I get him? Do you know if I killed the other guy?" Curt realized then that medical skill may have been able to repair a heart, but it could not change a heart.

In parenting, all we can do is our part. We can teach our children honesty, hard work, and compassion. We can guide our children with love, and we can do all in our power to help them become responsible adults, but we can't do it all. The rest is up to our children.

[WE'RE ALL STILL LEARNING]

If all of us were perfect parents living in a perfect world, none of this would be a concern. But we're not perfect, and we're certainly not in a perfect world. One mother said, "I wish I had known earlier what I know now. There is nothing like raising children to make you feel like a bumbling child yourself." All we can do is sincerely give it our best shot. It's OK to have highs and lows, and everything we say does not have to sound profound. Mistakes are allowed for both children and parents. They are part of learning and growing up for everyone.

The fact is, when young people see us stumble along at times and realize that we are not all-knowing, perfect parents, it often helps them to relate better to us. When we have "one of those days," it can help us feel more understanding and empathetic toward our teenagers. Mutual vulnerability can sometimes bring us closer.

One father was beside himself as he saw his bright and handsome son "throw it all away." The boy gave up on all that his father had hoped he would accomplish. The father and the boy's teachers tried to talk to him, but they were met with cold stares. The father felt frustrated: "That boy has more talent and ability in his little finger than I do in my whole body. But I can't do it for him. I'm afraid he will have to learn a few lessons the hard way."

The father knew that his son might be able to drop out of everything else, but he couldn't drop out of learning. All the boy had really managed to do was to select more difficult courses from the hardest teachers of all: experience and pain. These teachers give the test first and the lessons later. It is said that such a school is for fools, but we can understand when students enroll there. Haven't we all been through just such a class or two ourselves? Making painful mistakes is usually what motivates us to finally start thinking things through before we act. Such mistakes help us develop problem-solving skills. As hard as it may be to accept, some rebellion or disillusionment can even be healthy and necessary for growth, maturity, and internalization of values.

To those of you struggling with these problems, the secret is to hang in there. Do your best to help, nurture, and love your children, but also realize that your children still have their choices to make. Take some comfort in knowing you've tried your best to help inform and guide those choices, and when all you can do is still not enough, remember we're all still learning.

"Are we there yet?" Not quite. We've hit a snowstorm, and our trip has stalled. Visibility is limited, the wind is howling—and so are the kids. Suddenly, and by no fault of our own, we hit a patch of ice and slid off the roadway into a snow bank. We called a tow truck, but who knows when it'll get here. The situation is completely out of our control, and we need to patiently wait it out. We can still find happiness in this part of our journey by focusing on what we can control. We have plenty of gas, and the heater still works. We are warm. We can even find ways to be happy while waiting. We're still quite a ways from our destination, but we're doing the best we can. Family happiness is found when we focus on what we can control rather than what we can't—on road trips and when raising children.

[PRINCIPLES OF ACTION]

How can you find comfort when all you can do is still not enough? Here are some possibilities:

» **Hang In and Hang On:** Think of a time when you worked at something for a long time and finally saw it come to fruition. What lessons did you learn during that process?

» **Do Your Part:** How can defining your responsibilities help you feel more confident when working with others?

» **We're All Still Learning:** What have you learned recently? How can knowing that you're still learning affect your view of your struggling family member?

SHINE THE LIGHT

Brad remembers in high school when the picture of a new girl showed up in the wallet of his friend Steve. "Wow! Who is that?" he asked, examining the picture closely.

"Believe it or not, it's my cousin," Steve bragged. "We had a family get-together over the weekend, and she gave me that picture."

Brad spent the next week trying to figure out a way to be invited to the next family get-together. The cousin in the picture in Steve's wallet really was beautiful. She and Steve were around the same age and felt especially close to each other. Like Steve, she also had wonderful parents and a loving family.

Then things started to change. It wasn't anything that happened overnight—just small things that slowly turned into big things, and big things that soon became huge things. Throughout high school, the new pictures Steve would show Brad of his cousin were different somehow. She was still beautiful. It was just that her countenance was changed.

In the years that followed, the girl ultimately left her family and ran away. Her choice hurt the family deeply.

Steve, like everyone else in the family, felt a tremendous loss. He struggled with his cousin's decision and felt personally hurt and rejected. He missed her—not just her presence at the traditional get-togethers, but also how she used to be. He missed the girl who was once in his wallet. He said, "I kept thinking of the grief her parents were feeling. I thought about my own pain and wanted so much to do something— anything. I guess helplessness is the worst feeling of all. But I knew that there was one thing I could do, no matter what. I could still love her." Later, he wrote this song, dedicated to his cousin:

The road that you walk is so different from mine.
And things we believed you have left far behind.
You're turning from things that are tender to me
To follow a star that I never can see.
In all of your searching for answers and ends,
Did you ever consider the place you began?

For the table is set and there's bread to be broken,
Sweet words of forgiveness to be spoken all around.
And there's living water to quench all your thirsting.
And maybe the end of all your searching will be found.

As day follows day I have started to see
That love does not mean we will always agree.
I cannot pretend that I know how you feel.
All that I know is that I love you still.
No matter what roads you've traveled alone,
I just hope you know you can always come home.

So I'll set my love like a candle in the window
That someday in the distance you may see the light
And come home.

Few things are as warm and inviting as a candle in the window. However, when nights are cold and the window frosts over, it's easy to become discouraged and wonder if our little light will even be seen. It's easy to lose hope. But if we will keep the candle in place, then the heat of the flame will slowly melt a small circle in the frost. Our light will shine through into the darkness. And then, like Steve, we can hope that maybe someday the ones we pray for will see the light and come home. There is a Spanish saying that, when translated, says, "The most wonderful thing about happy endings is that sometimes they happen."

The secret is to remember that no matter how far away our children may appear at times, every person has the inner capacity to recall and respond to light and truth—and love.

[BIRDS WILL RETURN HOME]

In his book *Charity Never Faileth*, Vaughn J. Featherstone shared the following:

> Dr. Gustav Eckstein, one of the world's renowned ornithologists, worked in the same laboratory for over twenty-five years. He bred and crossbred species of birds, and kept meticulous records on the varieties and hybrids of birds in his laboratory. Each day when he would enter his laboratory, he would go down two or three stairs to the stereo. He would put on classical music and turn the volume up very loud. Then he would go about his work. The birds would sing along with the classical music. At the end of the day, about 5:30 p.m., he would turn off the stereo and leave for home.
>
> After twenty-five years, he had to hire a new custodian. One evening after Dr. Eckstein left the laboratory, the new custodian thought the place should be aired out, so he opened all the windows. The next morning when Dr. Eckstein went

into his laboratory he saw the open windows and noted that every bird had flown out during the night. He was devastated, his life's work ruined. By habit or instinct, he went to the stereo and turned the classical music up very loud. Then he sat down on the steps, put his head in his hands, and wept.

The strains of music carried out through the open windows, through the trees, and down the streets. In a few moments, Dr. Eckstein heard the fluttering of wings. He looked up and saw that the birds were beginning to come back into the laboratory through the open windows. "And," he reported, "every bird came back."[i]

Just like these birds, the wayward children of diligent parents will also come to realize that the very counsel of wise and loving parents they have rejected in the past is the thing that will ultimately save them. When no one else will stand by them, children will often return to the love of family and parents—the very people they once mistrusted and thought intolerant.

With this hope in mind, we can make it through any situation, no matter how difficult and impossible it may seem.

[ONE WOMAN'S STORY]

A woman we know shared this story about how she eventually found her way home:[ii]

I was married when I was nineteen. I married a man who was manic-depressive. If you will take the time in your life when you were most depressed and multiply that by one hundred, that's the way my husband used to get.

It wasn't too many months after we were married that I found him on the floor in the bathroom having taken an entire bottle of aspirin. Another time, he took every scrapbook I had made in my life into the backyard and burned them. I thought I could make things better if I had a child. When that little boy was a year and a half old, I was performing in a ballet. My husband called me offstage and said that there was an emergency. I rushed out to the car, and he put a gag in my mouth, bound my wrists and ankles, and drove off. He had a gun and threatened to kill me. It was horrible.

That was the beginning of a very low time in my life. My mother didn't know anything about what was going on. She just saw the external signs of her daughter deteriorating. One day, when I couldn't take it anymore, I rushed over to my mother's house with my little boy. I said, "Here, take him. I'm leaving."

I hate to admit it, but I left my son and I ran. I joined the Atlanta Ballet Company. My heart grew hard. I had been through so much trauma and pain with my husband that I never wanted to go home again.

Several months later, I received a letter from my mother. She had included a snapshot of my little son with his toy bunny rabbit. I was boarding with a family, and the daughter was playing a music box with the song "Sunrise, Sunset" from Fiddler on the Roof.

I set the picture aside and tried to block out the music by reading the newspaper. What I didn't realize was that it was Mother's Day. When I opened the paper there was this poem:

"Where are you going?" you'd say to him,
"And what are you going to do?"
And with a shy smile, he'd toddle outside
To slay a dragon for you.
Or perhaps there was a prince to be,
Or a lion to track to its lair.
For a little boy's life is a wondrous thing,
As long as his mother's there.

"Why do birds fly all in a flock?
How far are the stars from the ground?"
A thousand questions he'd ask of you,
A thousand answers you found.
"Please tell me what makes a puppy dog bark?
And why is the sky filled with air?"
For a little boy's life is a learning thing,
As long as his mother's there.

"Sing me a tune," he'd say to you.
"Sing me some soft lullabies."
And you'd sit by his bed for a moment or two,
Until slowly he'd close his eyes.
How quiet he'd be as you covered him up
And caressed his silken hair.
For a little boy's life is a peaceful thing,
As long as his mother's there.

"Don't cry," you'd say as you held him close,
When he'd fallen and hurt his head.
You held back a tear yourself, you know,
When you'd kissed the spot where it bled.
And his tears dried up, and the hurt went away,

Under your gentle care.
For a little boy's life is a loving thing,
As long as his mother's there.

And one day you'll look up, as the years speed by,
And I know it will seem to you
That he isn't a little boy anymore,
But a fine man, grown straight, tall, and true.
How fast they go, these little boy years.
Thank God you have them to share.
For though a little boy's life is a fleeting thing,
To a mother, it's always there.

That was a turning point for me. I packed up and went home—home to my mother and home to raise my son. Later, my second husband and I got married. At nineteen, my son went away to college. On the day I said farewell, I recited the above poem. That was the day the poem talked about. I looked up and saw that John wasn't a little boy anymore but a fine man, grown straight, tall, and true.

I'm grateful my mom never gave up on me. At a time in my life when things were the darkest, she set her love like a candle in the window, and somehow in the distance I saw the light and came home.

"Are we there yet?" No. We are still heading in the right direction, even though some family members may get lost, and it may take parents a long time to find those lost family members. Never lose hope. We can reach the destination, and we can get there together. When we do, we'll realize that it is worth it—not just because of where we finally end up, but because of how we have grown and all we have become because we were willing to take the trip.

[PRINCIPLES OF ACTION]

How can we help family members find the light guiding them home? Here are some suggestions:

» **Birds Will Return Home:** Think of Dr. Eckstein's experience with his birds. What can you learn from that experience that could help in your current situation?

» **One Woman's Story:** How can you place a "candle in the window" for struggling family members? How have others done that for you in the past?

[ENDNOTES]

i. Vaughn J. Featherstone, *Charity Never Faileth* (Salt Lake City: Deseret Book, 1980).

ii. Barbara Barrington Jones and Brad Wilcox, *Straight Talk for Parents: What Teenagers Wish They Could Tell You* (Salt Lake City: Deseret Book, 1994).

[CONCLUSION]

Jerrick and his family had a wonderful time in Colorado. They enjoyed being with family and made lots of new memories. Although the vacation was fun, it had to end. The family packed up the bags into their now dirty, dusty suburban, grabbed some food, and headed back home. Within an hour of leaving, every child was fast asleep. They were exhausted from all the hiking, playing games, and staying up late with cousins. Mom and Dad enjoyed their quiet time together while the children were asleep. The return trip home began much smoother than the trip away, but it didn't last for long.

After a few hours, the children began waking up, one by one, until Trevor was the last one asleep. He had spent a bit more time in the mountains than the rest of his siblings had, and he had hardly slept during the whole vacation. He still wanted to keep playing, but the vibrations of the car engine and the trees whipping past outside the window proved too much for this ten-year-old boy. He was out, and nothing could wake him. Nothing, that is, except his recurring motion sickness.

Maybe it was the curving, winding road; maybe it was the rapidly decreasing elevation; or maybe it was dehydration, but all of a sudden, Trevor woke up. "I don't feel too good," he groaned.

Mom looked back from her view in the passenger's seat, even though she knew what was going to happen. Trevor was turning pale green before her eyes, and quickly, too. This had happened before on family trips, so the family was prepared.

"Someone grab the bucket!" Mom pleaded, but it was too late.

Trevor lost it all. He was a mess, and the car now smelled horrible.

Slowly, once the shock of this drastic turn of events wore off, Dad started laughing. He may have been laughing because he was driving and didn't have to help clean Trevor off immediately. Whatever the reason, his laughter started a chain reaction among the whole family. Even Trevor joined in. Dad pulled over at the next rest stop, Trevor changed clothes, and the trip continued.

"Are we there yet?" Is this trip ever going to end? For Jerrick's family, their Colorado trip did come to an end, and they were able to get home safely. But their journey together as a family didn't end when that car pulled into the driveway. Our journeys through life with our family don't end either. We will never truly be "there," but our hope is that the eighteen principles in this book can help you be happier as a family. As parents, you can use these best-kept secrets of parenting to help your family grow closer together and find joy in the journey toward family happiness. The Principles of Action can serve as reviews as you map out where you've been and where you need to go to gain that greater family happiness. We hope you will refer back to them and see the benefits that will come to your family.

Our ultimate goal isn't to arrive any place in particular; our goal is to enjoy the trip. It's the road we're on, not the destination, that's most important—the road to family happiness. That's the best-kept secret of all.

[ADDITIONAL SOURCES]

Some of the material in this book has been adapted from the following previously published books and articles:

Jones, Barbara Barrington and Brad Wilcox. *Straight Talk for Parents: What Teenagers Wish They Could Tell You.* Salt Lake City: Deseret Book, 1994.

Porter, Marc and Brad Wilcox. "Cool-aid." *The New Era*, 27.6 (1997): 10-11.

Robbins, Jerrick. "It's OK to Cry." *Lessons from my Parents: 100 Shared Moments that Changed Our Lives.* Ed. Michelle Robbins (Sanger, CA: Familius, 2013). Page 247.

Wilcox, Brad. "Being Friends with Your Parents." In R. Wright Ed., *Friends Forever.* Salt Lake City: Bookcraft, 1996. 25-37.

———. "Closed Doors and Open Windows." *Ensign*, 23.12 (1993): 58.

———. "Getting Over Feeling Underappreciated." *Ensign*, 34.3 (2004): 46-49.

———. "Honestly, There's No Better Way." *Ensign*, 22.9 (1992): 30-34.

———. "If We Can Laugh at It, We Can Live with It." *Ensign*, 30.3 (2000): 26-30.

———. "May I Have This Dance?" *The New Era*, 9.7 (1979): 46-49.

———. "My Toothless Teacher." *The New Era*, 8.5 (1978): 6-7.

———. "Why Write It?" *Ensign*, 29.9 (1999): 56-57.

———. "Work Enough for Two." *Ensign*, 25.1 (1995): 63.

[ABOUT FAMILIUS]

Welcome to a place where mothers are celebrated, not compared. Where heart is at the center of our families, and family at the center of our homes. Where boo boos are still kissed, cake beaters are still licked, and mistakes are still okay. Welcome to a place where books—and family—are beautiful. Familius: a book publisher dedicated to helping families be happy.

[VISIT OUR WEBSITE: WWW.FAMILIUS.COM]

Our website is a different kind of place. Get inspired, read articles, discover books, watch videos, connect with our family experts, download books and apps and audiobooks, and along the way, discover how values and happy family life go together.

[JOIN OUR FAMILY]

There are lots of ways to connect with us! Subscribe to our newsletters at www.familius.com to receive uplifting daily inspiration, essays from our Pater Familius, a free ebook every month, and the first word on special discounts and Familius news.

[BECOME AN EXPERT]

Familius authors and other established writers interested in helping families be happy are invited to join our family and contribute online content. If you have something important to say on the family, join our expert community by applying at: www.familius.com/apply-to-become-a-familius-expert

[GET BULK DISCOUNTS]

If you feel a few friends and family might benefit from what you've read, let us know and we'll be happy to provide you with quantity discounts. Simply email us at specialorders@familius.com.

Website: www.familius.com
Facebook: www.facebook.com/paterfamilius
Twitter: @familiustalk, @paterfamilius1
Pinterest: www.pinterest.com/familius

The most important work

you ever do will be within

the walls of your own home.

CPSIA information can be obtained at www.ICGtesting.com
Printed in the USA
BVOW03s1222080814

361821BV00003B/9/P